Robert Ing

Dr. Robert Ing is a real life Forensic Intelligence Specialist. For over 20 years his survival and success in his profession has been the result of his ability to "cut to the chase" and take the politically incorrect road of asking and contemplating the hard options. He is a man that considers the unthinkable whether it be preparing for disaster or being an advisor in an incident investigation.

A regularly featured guest on most major North American news networks, host of several public television specials and his own current events program, it is very difficult for any television viewer not to see his face and wonder where they had seen him before.

He offers this overview of this, his 13th book:

"At first glance it may appear that this book is simply a collection of essays, dramatized subjective accounts of real events and editorials where the names have been changed. However, what this book is really about is perception.

All too often people take for granted the things they have or believe for the things they have been convinced that they need or should believe as a result of social persuasion for the herd. Faith without work is dead and truth without proof is fatal.

This is the book that will make you consider the world around you, cause some doubt in your life and give you a window on technology that you thought had very little impact on your life."

CHATTER BEYOND
THE FRINGE

Robert Ing, DSc, DLitt, FAPSc

CHATTER BEYOND THE FRINGE

Robert Ing, DSc, DLitt, FAPSc

iUniverse, Inc.
New York Lincoln Shanghai

CHATTER BEYOND THE FRINGE

iUniverse books may be ordered through booksellers or by contacting:

iUniverse
2021 Pine Lake Road, Suite 100
Lincoln, NE 68512
www.iuniverse.com
1-800-Authors (1-800-288-4677)

ISBN: 978-0-595-45589-8 (pbk)
ISBN: 978-0-595-69819-6 (cloth)
ISBN: 978-0-595-89890-9 (ebk)

Printed in the United States of America

This book is dedicated to
Diamond Michelle Ing
Samuel Robert Matthew Ing
Robert & Elizabeth Campbell (1899–1981 & 1892–1966)

Contents

ACKNOWLEDGEMENTS

A belief of the old religion was that people are introduced into the life of an individual to teach, guide, make them stronger, or in order for them to meet their destiny. It is a fact that in this life the average individual will personally know anywhere from 252 to 396 people. Here are some of those individuals without whom I may have never survived being in front of the camera or on the stage of life.

Azure Brown
Shaun Campbell
Len Cooper (1928–2003)
Victoria Grant
Michelle Henry
Debra Lee
Christine Lewis
Sid Lorraine (1905–1989)
Bruce Posgate (1900–1990)

SPECIAL THANKS & HONORABLE MENTION

A.R. Brownsburger
Yolanda V. Burgess
Channel 81 Television
Coach Bambi
Coffee Zone
Fuel Fitness Clubs
Daniele M. Gallimore
Professor Alec B.R. (Lexmor) Morrison (1903–1984)
Julie Saggers Photography

IN REMEMBRANCE
AND IN HONOR

"While they sleep we are out there.
When they sit down to dinner we are out there.
When it is raining and cold we are out there.
When it is our child's birthday we are out there.

There is room for error in their jobs, in ours there is none.
When they tell their family, "I'll see you tonight" they will.
When we do, we can only pray that we will.

At their jobs they strive to succeed.
In ours, we strive to survive.
In the headlines it is not what good we have done
but how much better it could have been done.
Most of what we see and do will never make the evening news.
Most of what we see and do, we will never talk about because most
would not understand
and others would simply not believe.
Silence is our trade and we are duty bound to keep what we see
with us.

*A hard day for them may be having the boss or client chew them
out,
or perhaps getting that new car scratched.
For us, it is seeing someone die and not being able to do
anything to save them.
For us, it is knowing that someone is perpetrating evil and not
having the resources to intervene.*

*When they are afraid they call us,
when we are afraid we carry on.*

*We are the first to know,
the first to go in and the last to leave.*

*When they eat with their families,
we eat alone.*

*When they sleep with their spouses,
we sleep alone.*

*We do what has to be done.
We do it to maintain right.
We do it to ensure safety and security, today and tomorrow."*

—Anonymous

"On 6 January XXXVI A.S., sheep in the regalia of goats sat to hear the petitions of objection on behalf of people seeking justice and the upholding of the constitutional rights of every citizen to democracy. The sheep in goats regalia were deaf with their own pretentiousness and did not stand, not a single one but all lay down as sheep ultimately do. This marked the true beginning of the end of the greatest symbol of democracy the world had ever known and the erosion of freedom for her people."

CHATTER BEYOND THE FRINGE
Robert Ing, DSc, DLitt, FAPSc

Chatter:

[Intelligence Term] A term used to describe voice or data transmission activity on a communication line or channel under surveillance.

Fringe:

[Intelligence Term] An area outside of the target surveillance area that can be monitored, overheard, or observed.

NOTICE TO THE READER

The following chapters are based on the professional experiences and cases of Dr. Robert Ing. The accounts represented have been dramatized and the dates, names, organizations, agencies and locations have been changed. Characters portrayed in these accounts do not necessarily represent any individual either living or dead. The accounts in this book do not violate any non-disclosure agreements, or oaths of secrecy entered into by the author with any individual, corporation, sovereign nation, government or other legal entity. Technical details represented in these accounts are for informational background purposes only and lack sufficient specification for execution. The author, publisher, their agents and distributors will not be held liable or accountable for the use or misuse of information contained in this book.

CHAPTER 1

━━━━━━━━━ ▼ ━━━━━━━━━

The Briefing:
A SITUATION REPORT
(SitRep), ESSAY AND
PERSONAL RANT

"It is far better for me to take a stand, so that you may know the man I truly am than to simply sit quietly on my hands"

—Robert Ing

Welcome to the briefing. I appreciate the fact that you decided to sit in today. Some of the things we are going to discuss here are not meant to be taken personally but rather are simply observations of different situations. These observations are based on information that has been gathered, analyzed and filtered over an extended period of time, to the point, well, that they may even give the veneer of being subjective observations. But we both know better, or don't we?

My business is forensic intelligence and I have been at it for more than 20 years. Imagine a world where there were no computers, no DNA, no cross-referencing of information; this was the world of forensic science that I began my career in. In the early days I started out in the areas of skeletal identification and fingerprinting but soon moved on to what would become my own professional niche. Now, I know that you are thinking, corpses and fingerprint dust, but that's not what I do. Forensic Intelligence deals with the acquisition, analysis and protection of information and evidence that is the result of a criminal act, and the identification of potential crime risks. Forensic Intelligence endeavors to associate committed crimes to specific perpetrators through in-depth analysis. Within Forensic Intelligence are the functions of Counter-Terrorism, and Espionage and Criminal Risk Management, which involves the acquisition and analysis of intelligence data in order to provide recommendations on reducing terrorist, espionage and criminal threat levels.

O.K., now that I have given you a definition that every lawyer would salivate at, let me cut to the chase. I look at the facts and evidence, mostly in electronic and paper form and from that I establish links to the alleged perpetrator. Where no crime has actually taken place, I use this information to figure out if there is the potential risk or threat of a criminal act waiting to happen. The ability to understand what someone may be planning, or the possible security hole that poses a risk is particularly important when it comes to the acts of Espionage, Terrorism and Organized Criminal Activity. My area of specialty is Technology Crime and within that area I focus on espionage risk management, identity theft, privacy, surveillance and computer security. So what do all these things have in common? They are all commonly used and violated by spies, terrorists and organized criminals as a target, instrument, aid or propagator of their illegal activity.

My first real job was with a major metropolitan police department followed by service in the armed forces and subsequent investigative and security assignments in both the public and private sector. It is a fact that not more than 20% of espionage cases against Top 1000 companies ever get reported to public law enforcement. They do this because they cannot open themselves to the potential damage of falling share prices, decreased public confidence and due diligence litigation issues if the word ever got out that they fell victim to spies or even worse terrorists. 72% of corporations that have not taken measures to manage corporate espionage risk and suffer a loss have typically gone out of business within 2 years. There are many other problems that could arise that I have purposely omitted and all one has to do is to use their imagination to consider what other entities other than multinational corporations may have been behind this proverbial eight ball. The multinational corporate community tends to call in private security advisors, do damage control and pursue civil litigation as a cautious option. This is where I come in. I am the private citizen who works as a forensic intelligence specialist or as the security advisor. Many former employers and colleagues have referred to me as a "fixer" or "troubleshooter."

When it comes to doing my job, I prefer stealth rather than flash but because of my "in your face" get the job done and "always out front" attitude I have won myself the reputation of being unmanageable by those who prefer to manage from a posh office as opposed to the field. However, those who do deem me unmanageable still call me in and on occasion have sent me across the globe to take command, control and to be the back-shop equalizer. I am by no means the best in the field but as a result of my diverse experience, numerous news media appearances and higher than average public profile, I have been considered by many to be one of the many leaders in this discipline. Due to this notoriety, I have had the privilege of training and working with some of the bravest men and women in public and private law enforcement and security throughout the world. In my life I have dined and partied with presidents, prime ministers, diplomats, the creme de la creme of society and have had soup with the people in the hood. I have traveled the world, seen the best and the worst of it. I have also witnessed a great deal regarding the human condition and as a result feel that it is important to present to you my view of how I see some aspects of our world. What you see happening firsthand in the streets of your community is a microcosm of the condition of the greater macrocosm in our world.

No matter what century we live in, the proverbial, "times have really changed" is simply the motto of humankind for all time. However, the motivation of our species can be summed up in three words: money, power and politics. No matter who you are, what you do or who you do it for, you will find that it either directly or indirectly touches the concept of money, power or politics.

Generally, people regardless of who they are, what they believe and where they come from all really want three basic things. They want food, shelter and clothing for themselves and their families. They want the security in knowing that they will have and can get these things. In the Western world we accept these things in abundance, as a given right, and overlook them for what they really are—a privilege. Once people feel secure about basic food, shelter and clothing they tend to turn their attention on acquiring all kinds of other things. Regardless of their station in life, people use what they have in the form of money, power and politics in one way or another to acquire these and other things.

When it comes to money there are only five ways to acquire it. You can sell goods, services or your labor for it; you can inherit or be born into it; you can win it; you can steal it; or you can invest an initial amount with someone who may earn you more by doing any of the previously mentioned activities on your behalf. Fortunately, people with money are not all powerful, because as I am sure you have come to realize that there are a great deal of people with money that are so out of tune with the real world that if they did not have their money, they would never be able to survive doing the daily things the average person has to do to live.

Power can be in the form of authority or position; knowledge or information; or having control of something of value excluding money. People of power use and broker their power for money. People of power are not necessarily monetarily wealthy and could be just as financially well off as the average individual. Power people use their intellect to broker deals, sell and acquire information or exercise control over resources of value. To remain powerful one must constantly be vigilant so as not to broker too much power in the form of information or control for money lest they end up an outcast. Balance is the key to power.

Politics in this sense does not refer to political parties, elections and who one votes for. Politics refers to one's ability to associate with and influence those that can further his or her own goals. In order to succeed in politics you personally must have a certain je ne sais quoi on how to walk into a room filled with strangers and at the end of the night walk out with at least half of these people's contact information and identify them as a money, power or politics player. The ability to talk with and convince people that you are sincere whether you really are or not, is a talent for some, or an acquired skill for others. Some have it, some don't. Needless to say, this is one talent or skill those in the theatre of politics must have in order to be in the game for the next round.

In the business world an executive's true worth is not measured by education or experience but the size of their personal business address book. The more contacts a person has, the greater their ability to associate with and influence those who may have money, power or have similar political agendas. The average person will personally know anywhere from 252 to 396 people during the course of their entire life. A real political player must personally know an average of 468 people. This process must start at no later than their 36th birthday. They must be extremely selective with whom they choose to get to know personally during the course of their lifetime in order to cultivate professionally beneficial connections. In the game of politics you either know people on the inside, or you have someone who does. If you have neither of these, you will have the political longevity of a lemur. People who know how to play politics; that is work a room, know who to contact or the time to call in a favor when something is afoot, and are able to accomplish an unpopular act while maintaining their own popularity are true masters of the game. Those who deal in politics are the brokers of change, both good and bad. They are backed by money people and armed with information from power people in order to put fourth their political agendas.

To some extent, even the average individual dabbles in the money, power and politics game. When was the last time you offered to do something for someone in exchange for cash, or bartered—negotiated something for a better deal, or called up someone you knew to ask them to do something only they could do for you? These situations reflect money, power and politics respectively. And you thought you didn't play the game. We all do, and most think of it as survival.

Take a walk with me downtown. See those buildings. See all those names on the buildings. There are buildings with the names of banks, insurance companies, health care outfits, car companies, hotel chains, and financial brokers. You know how they got their names up there? They did it because they had information that was so good, that it convinced people to do business with them, and even helped them make the right choices of where to put their money, and be politically correct so they could grow their business without stepping on powerful toes. Someone once said that information is power, but that is simply not true. If it were that would mean the most powerful people in the world would be librarians and I.T. (information technology) administrators!

Information is only as powerful as your ability to apply it. If you can't apply it, you may not be powerful, but if you can sell it to someone who can apply it, you might become very wealthy. The next best thing to having information in your personal possession is knowing where to find it (knowledge). If you were not born into wealth, have an average to below average intellect and have no contacts that can connect you to a situation where you can earn a reasonable living, there is only one viable option for you if you are really going to survive and have a life in this world. Learn what type of information people need, leave no stone unturned on finding sources of information, learn how to put it in a way people can understand and sell it to them. Sell it to them for real cash, then go back and do it again.

The average person acquires most of their information through the eyes and experiences (accounts) of others. They will get this information from the broadcast, film, video, print media, the Internet and from recollections of friends and relatives who have obtained it from all the sources I have previously mentioned, and so on, and so on, and so on … well you get the idea. What was that I said about objective observations under a veneer of subjectivity?

Elementary school children have a game where about a dozen of them line up or stand in a circle. The first child is given a secret to whisper in the ear of the next child and so on down the line to the last child. The strange thing about it is the last child only has a thirty-three percent chance of getting the entire original message. How do you get your news of what is happening in the world today? Do you truly believe that you are being told everything?

The world is filled with people who accept and never question what they are told by the mainstream media, their government and the alternative media. For most people, the acceptance of what they perceive as fact is based on their own limited life experiences, personal beliefs, popular culture and regrettably what is convenient for them to believe at the time. Oh yes, and on the amount of information the teller is willing to provide without censorship and bias within the constraints of time or editorial space. The ability to use these variables to one's advantage in shaping the perception of the average citizen is nothing short of information warfare or information terrorism, (depending on what side of the issues you are on) at its most basic level.

Have you looked at a real paper version of a daily newspaper lately? Now, don't cheat and look at one on the Internet but actually think of the last time you held one in your hand. Do you realize that the information in that newspaper, today's edition of that newspaper contains more information than you would ever be exposed to in your entire lifetime if you lived four hundred years ago? It's a fact and that is just a daily newspaper. We actually live in an age where we as individuals are literally flooded with so much information that the average individual finds it difficult to digest large chunks of single source information at one time. People are conditioned as a result of this info-environment to expect and receive sensory information from constantly changing multiple sources. If you don't believe me, consider the number of people that you know that suffer from short attention spans, are unable to focus on one thing at a time and are constant channel hoppers when it comes to television or radio. You probably know a lot more of these individuals than you did five, ten or twenty years ago.

Up until about 1980, major corporate executives had executive assistants conduct preliminary research and gather information for upcoming projects. Today, the same corporate executives have their executive assistants sift through, filter and summarize literally gigabytes of reports, e-mails, and other forms of information. In a world that relies on information, those that have the information conduits can and do direct the path it will take. Those with access to multiple information conduits will and do filter it in order to meet their requirement or justify their agenda.

Enter my twisted idea of a contemporary Zen Buddhist riddle. A boy moves into a neighborhood and is shown by his new classmates how to get to school from his house. The boy walks the route each day to and from school with the total trip lasting 45 minutes. Having made this trek for the better part of a year, the boy one day is confronted with massive road and street construction which forces him to double back and try to find an alternate route to school. He does, after much angst, only to find the new route is 15 minutes shorter!

From this story we can establish that the boy in the very beginning accepted as empirical fact, presented by his classmates that this was the only route to school. The alternate route was not known to him or even perhaps his classmates. As this route was not known, did this mean it did not exist? In the context of the window or circle of reality of the boy and his classmates, one could easily say yes, it did not exist, and therefore was not real to them. It posed no advantage or threat to them at that time. However, in the big picture, to you and I, we know better.

When subjective reality is accepted as truth and people blindly buy into the concept that the truth shall set them free, they voluntarily become their own jailers and slaves to a world beyond their control. The only way for an individual to be truly free and be in charge of their own destiny is to question everything and before taking action, consider the personal impact and long term consequences to themselves and others of such action. At the end of the day, each individual must accept full responsibility for their own actions whether time proves their decision to be appropriate or inappropriate.

Now, here's the punch line. Today, there are high level people, influential people, powerful people, well intentioned professional people charged with the national security interests of all of us who are like the boy and his classmates. If it is not in the book, if it is not an identified security vulnerability, it does not exist. If it is not politically correct it cannot be discussed or acknowledged. How absurd and sad. It is not my intention, to point fingers or name names because this would not cure or fix what has become the popular security theories of the day, and their high profile, marketing spin doctored trained proponents. However, consider the facts and acts of terrorism, guerilla warfare and organized professional crime in our world today. Consider all the resources, the training, the technology, and the lessons we have learned from the tragic history of our world. Don't you find it beyond belief that some criminal and terrorist acts against our civilized world; some acts that take months of planning, still seem to not even cause a "blip" on the radar screen until after they have been executed and members of the innocent, unknowing public are sacrificed. Even more unbelievable are the untold millions of dollars allocated as a knee jerk reaction to such events to protect us, from and to find those responsible for such acts. Yet with all this, it seems that finding and neutralizing the single significant primary perpetrator, a man or woman is beyond the scope of everything that has been put in place. Perhaps one day, an epiphany will happen when it will be realized that organized professional criminals, guerillas and terrorists do not follow or could care less about what we recognize as standard casebook exploits and modus operandi. A possible but highly improbable scenario, at least in this lifetime.

During my appearances on national television and at conferences, I have clearly demonstrated on several occasions the ease at which targeted information can be obtained from virtually any Internet or Intranet connected computer, only to have some established experts cry "smoke and mirrors" or "illusions" as opposed to understanding the real security threat to every citizen. For the past twenty years I had attempted to lobby the corporate sector to allocate better funding for internal security budgets and advanced security training for their people but still to this day, frontline security staff in corporate North America are still the lowest paid of risk management staff in relation to the value of the assets and lives they must protect.

Furthermore, national legislation must be in place that all private security guards pass a criminal background check, meet the professional certification requirement as a Certified Protection Officer, established by the International Foundation for Protection Officers (IFPO) or as a Certified Physical Security Professional, established by the American Society for Industrial Security (ASIS) and are remunerated at a rate reflective of their responsibility as a frontline risk management professional. Private security guards play a key role in managing terrorist and criminal risk in our communities. This is crucial for the safety and security of themselves and those who depend upon them.

In the mid 1990s, I had authored a paper and lectured on custom instructive code (Trojan) viruses that were, and still are, virtually undetectable. This computer Trojan virus is capable of searching for specific file names or keywords on an infected computer and then e-mailing the files back to its originator. In 2005, I demonstrated on live television how easy it was, to locate and access computers without firewalls and to extract credit card numbers using only a laptop computer with a wireless connection and modified web crawler—search program. These are not conjuring tricks but are real threats to individuals, companies and our national security.

There is an international computer underground of organized criminals and privateers; individuals who act alone and steal information to order for a price. Their targets range from personal information, research data and client lists to access codes and architectural plans. They operate below the security radar screen for the most part, using methodologies and processes that barely receive any mention in the accepted Internet or network security "grails" of the day. Personal information obtained today by an organized criminal or terrorist for the purpose of identity theft may not be utilized until a year or more after its acquisition. This is the world of technological espionage. Sorry, you won't get this information in your next professional security certification credit course. Having said this, on a positive note, there are people that know and have the technology to catch some of these individuals. Some of them I have had the privilege and honor of serving with. While others choose to work alone, tracking, monitoring and stopping these perpetrators for their private clientele. In the professional security business there is an often quoted but seldom heeded axiom, that being, "Security is a process." Security is not a static thing and must be proactively adaptable if it is to be of any real value in saving lives, privacy and property.

We fear the unknown and the things we don't understand or that are different to our own concept of the world. In the wild, animals will not typically venture into the unknown and if faced with fear would rather retreat, and will only fight for survival; defense or food. The human animal however, will plot or act to destroy that which causes him or her fear in the absence of rational facts that would make the unknown, known. It is this emotion based irrational behavior that causes knee jerk response national security policy to the detriment of our already fragile democracy and the individual freedoms fought for and earned by our forebears that are enjoyed by each one of us.

Governments and corporations spend untold millions of dollars on security initiatives that look good, offer a level of hollow intimidation through technology most people don't understand but offer little or no real protection against future threats. One of the greatest security faux pas of our time is the knee jerk reaction of beefing up or increasing physical visible security measures after an incident occurs. This is generally an unnecessary expense, creates a false sense of security and provides the politically correct impression that something is being done. This is not to say that increasing visible physical security should never be an option, but rather that it should be one of several options that have been pre-qualified based on an analysis of what started the problem in the first place. Just because the computer containing sensitive information is locked in a room at the beginning of the shift and it is still physically there at the end of the shift, with no unauthorized access attempts does not mean it is secure or has not been breached.

The act of managing risk or prevention consists of only three processes; that of reducing or negating the risk at its source, early detection/monitoring, and incident response. Adding more visible security resources will be of no use if the original core vulnerability has not been addressed. I know that this sounds like common sense but if you follow news reports on crime and acts of terrorism around the world, you will soon realize that in some cases, someone missed this simple consideration. If we are to manage crime and terrorist risk in our society, we must identify our vulnerabilities and implement strategies and processes that address these issues head on. We do not need and cannot afford action on these issues to be referred to a committee or study group of individuals that live in the best neighborhoods, have above average levels of personal security and will produce a report with recommendations that may be implemented over the course of time. It is unfortunate that quite often national security policies and measures are executed as a result of political and obscure agendas. If you don't believe me, ask yourself why politicians, our lawmakers— the people we elect to make and debate decisions on our safety and security can never give a straight yes or no answer to a vital safety or security question. You should also ask yourself why is it that every time a criminal act is committed against a free democratic society that the response is ultimately to assert more control over and restrict the rights and freedoms of that same society.

In our world today, there are some unspeakable but irrefutable axioms. The major governments of our world, including ours, could very easily eliminate poverty within their own borders. All they would have to do is to give every citizen; man, woman and child the equivalent to 1 million dollars in the form of a non-transferable, no cash redeemable credit during their lifetime, that could only be applied towards food, housing, clothing and education. This would not be a dole or a handout, but an investment in the future of humankind. People could truly excel at the talents and abilities they have for the betterment of their country and the world. This would not only eradicate poverty but also many incentives to consider a life of crime as a way of survival. It would stimulate the economy, help small businesses and communities. If you think this would be a great amount of money to come up with, think again the next time these governments seem to allocate or find millions of dollars, at the drop of a hat for a politically correct initiative of the day, while people struggle to make ends meet in our neighborhoods.

As long as we have poverty and a class known as the working poor in our country and the inability to effectively deliver the basic necessities to every citizen, our government should not be directly involved in providing financial aid outside our borders while our own suffer. As good citizens of the world and members of international aid organizations such as the International Red Cross, Amnesty International and the United Nations to name a few, we will help those in other countries who cannot help themselves due to lack of resources, understanding, social justice and political instability. However, we must ensure that we put our citizens, those who contribute to our country through their communities, first and foremost. Each day many parents in our cities are faced with tough decisions. Unfortunately, these decisions are whether to use their last five dollar bill to buy food for their children or to use it as a partial payment towards an overdue utility bill before it is disconnected. These people have jobs but simply do not earn enough to support their families or themselves. They may even work two or three minimum wage jobs, and are robbed of the valuable family time many of us take for granted, in exchange for trying to earn enough to provide food, clothing and shelter. This happens every day, in every city of our country while many with the power to change the situation do nothing. This is not acceptable.

The Armed Forces must be deployed and trained to defend our country, its borders and conduct disaster relief and emergency service operations. The Armed Forces must not be used to invade or police foreign nations. Our sons and daughters should not risk their lives or die for any action less than the direct defense or security of our nation. The men and women whether commissioned officers or non-commissioned officers in our military deserve better representation in, and an understanding of the challenges they face each day in executing their duties by the politicians that make up our government. It should be a mandatory requirement that a U.S. Defense Secretary or Canadian Minister of Defense have to his or her career experience, honorable regular (fulltime) military service as a prerequisite to appointment. It is always amazing and dare I say an act of cowardice when politicians can send our sons and daughters on military missions overseas, in many cases to risk their lives with little or no logistical support while they themselves go home to their sons and daughters. When asked if their sons or daughters would enlist for such a noble military action as they have defended it in the media time and time again, they seem to shrug their shoulders and simply walk away. The people in our Armed Forces deserve our respect and need the support of our politicians.

Immigration policy in our country is yet another sad issue. Did you know that our country goes to great lengths to paint a very rosy picture of our economy and job market in order to attract foreign professionals such as medical doctors, engineers, scientists and others. However, once such a foreign professional has landed, they soon discover that there exists a glass barrier that prohibits or restricts them from using their skills and experience to acquire employment. That glass barrier is American or Canadian work experience. While I am sure that human physiology, science and mathematics must be the same anywhere on our planet, this glass barrier has been used to literally put on the beach, some of the greatest foreign minds of our time. It's almost as though a conspiracy existed to drive these foreign intellectuals into the low wage, unskilled labor sector while they await the 3 or more years to qualify as a practicing professional, in order for our nation to have an intelligent low wage labor force to help our country better compete in world markets.

To understand this tragedy and waste of resources, one does not have far to go but the local employment center, hop in a taxi in a major metropolitan city or speak with the office cleaning staff. There you may be surprised to find a research scientist, medical doctor or electrical engineer. Another problem is the lack of a pre-requisite that potential immigrants to our country either demonstrate a functional fluency in our national language or agree to master it and pass a functional fluency exam before they settle in our country. Let's be honest, if a person cannot read, write or speak our national language, how can they personally survive in our society, let alone be a contributing member of our community. Unfortunately, we have people in our country that simply do not speak, read or write our national language. As a result they only socialize and survive in their own small ethnic community. This puts them at a disadvantage as they are isolated from many services available to the mainstream population and are often subject to illegal employment practices such as wages far below the legal minimum, poor and unsafe working and housing conditions. If we are to extend an invitation to people to immigrate, we must be willing to ensure that our system is designed to utilize and maximize their skills and experience to the benefit of our country and the world. We also owe it to those we invite to ensure that they are functionally literate in order that they may succeed in their new country and contribute their fair share.

Immigration policy must be based on a mutually beneficial relationship both for the potential immigrant and our nation. If there is no direct benefit for both parties, immigration to our country must be refused.

The concept of externally applied ethics, morality, law and order on an individual is far from absolute in creating a safe, secure and peaceful community. Externally applied controls for the communal good only have an impact of 33% on what can and does occur. For example, we can keep an eye on, or lock up bad people but it is impossible to do this for every bad apple, or maintain this vigilance all of the time. Furthermore, we cannot legislate common sense, responsibility or ethics any more than we can make a law that will prevent a crime. The remainder 67% of the equation rests solely with the individual. The only thing that stands between you committing murder, rape, assault or robbery is you. The only thing that ultimately keeps you from getting murdered, raped, assaulted or robbed is the personal restraint that others exercise upon themselves. This restraint either yours or each individual you encounter varies in degree with each negative and positive individual issue. If we are to foster a safer, more secure and peaceful community; we must begin with cultivating responsibility in individuals at an early age and continue throughout their entire life. Responsibility, intelligence and individuality are the characteristics that lead to an ethical, moral and law abiding society.

One of the major concerns in our inner cities is crime and our youth. This is a complex and serious problem. Today, many of our youth have no sense of their history, their culture, their roots. As a result, their existence is based on the misconception that they are here and everything begins and ends with them. They feel alone and need to be a part of a community. They often feel that they have no future and have no past. For many this turns out to be a gang or mischievous affiliations with other peers with a similar lack of knowing who they are and their history. Pop culture media does not help these youth as they are exposed to video images where every tough guy gets the girls, the money, the jewelry, the luxury car, and working for a living is for fools. Even more disturbing is the message to young males that girls are sex objects, woman are temporal trophies and the advice to young girls is that seduction is the best way to get money, jewelry and a sports car. To make matters worse, even the parents of some of these youngsters were they themselves dropped into life the same way with the same misplaced values. If you are a parent, you must talk to your children about their history, their culture, their ancestors. If you don't know this, work together with your children to do some research. Talk to older family members, read some books, watch documentaries, do a family tree. Let your children know that they are a living legacy. Teach and guide them in truly knowing where they came from and who they are. The most valuable family heirloom you can hand down through generation to generation is the history and culture of your family. With this knowledge will come self-respect and what will follow is respect for others. Instill within your sons and daughters a sense of responsibility, honor, personal value and the fact that all are not equal but each individual is truly unique.

Each year our cities become more and more ethnically diverse. So does the ethnicities of those who perpetrate crime in our communities. Unfortunately, every time an ethnically visible person commits a crime, they not only do a great disservice to themselves but also to their entire community. Although politically incorrect, the reality is that in the backs of the minds of mainstream society, every ethnic and non-ethnic group have their own criminal stereotype. Whenever a news photograph of a criminal that fits that particular stereotype is published, it simply reinforces this misconceived belief as fact. There are good and bad in all ethnicities and cultural groups. However, if a particular community has a problem, it should be that community's leaders that take the first pre-emptive, proactive role in coming up with solutions. Then, armed with a strategy, local lawmakers and government should be approached for input, feedback and support. Too many times, ethnic communities will simply wait for those in power to take the lead or approach the situation expecting government to take care of it. Who better than the community involved to spearhead the solution to a problem in its population? In any ethnic or culturally diverse community, there should be a mayor's advisory council with true representatives of these communities and members of the community emergency, law enforcement and social services. The advisory council should be used as a vehicle to identify issues and concerns, and as a means of finding solutions by consensus. At the end of the day not everyone may be pleased with some of the outcomes, but as long as there is dialogue and open communication, good practical solutions will always be a possibility.

The greatest moments and gifts that my father gave me were our monthly journeys downtown to a bookstore. At the age of 9, I made a lot of discoveries about the world just browsing the books on display. I didn't really read them but just read a few passages, looked at the illustrations and photographs. My favorite sections were the science and technology shelves. During a visit I came across a book called "The CET Study Guide" by Richard Glass. It was an electronics book that outlined study material for a Certified Electronics Technician exam. Oddly enough, later on in life, I ended up writing and passing this very exam, and later served on the board as Chairman of the Electronics Technicians Association and as a Director-at-Large on the board of the International Society of Certified Electronics Technicians; the two organizations that administer the CET program worldwide. I even had the honor and privilege of personally meeting Richard (Dick) Glass, President of ETA and working with him. It is the little things that you do with your children that will inspire and shape them. Perhaps the things you may not even be aware of. Take the time to do something with your children, talk to them, influence them but most important do it now, before it's too late.

Public Libraries are one of the last influences we have to maintain a civilized society. The modern day Public Library offers special interest community programs for children to adults, literacy programs, computer access and access to a myriad of books. As hard as it may seem to comprehend to some in this country, not every child or adult has or can afford a computer, the ability to buy the latest copy of their favorite magazine or pay for a reading program for their kids. Public Libraries do all this on a daily basis and more for over a third of our nation's population. Public Libraries are truly the great equalizer when it comes to equal access to knowledge for all. Public Library system funding is an issue that we must ensure is maintained if we as a society are to provide equal access to educational resources for all. As well, regular community recreation and special interest programs for youth have proven crucial in shaping our children to be upstanding citizens and reducing the risk of them getting into trouble. I owe my interest in science to my grade 3 teacher, Mr. A.R. Brownsberger, who between the roles of being school teacher and ad hoc school librarian took the time to introduce me (and others in class) to analogue computers, aviation and meteorology. Librarians and teachers do have an impact on how our children and youth will focus their energies as they go through life. We must make it second nature in the minds of our youth to choose understanding over violence, and intellectual expression over weapons.

Health care funding in our country is too little in the wrong place. With cut backs and general mismanagement we have seen emergency rooms closed at some hospitals, bed availability reduced and a general lack of keeping patients informed in delivering services to them. Many patients find that when they get referred to a specialist, it is often they who must maintain a vigilance with telephone calls and follow-ups otherwise they could very well fall off the radar screen. A major problem is really the patients! Many patients will go to the emergency or demand to see a doctor for minor ailments such as the common cold or other conditions that could clear up in a matter of three days. The patient really isn't at fault personally, because they are simply fearing the worst. However, these patients do slow down the health care delivery system to those that really need it as a matter of life and death, and they also increase the cost of health care delivery. The solution is very simple. Our government should allocate more funding to public education regarding health awareness and disease prevention. While there are currently many excellent but under-funded programs, they fall short in making a real dent with the mainstream public. We have to teach our citizens about preventive medicine, disease prevention, nutrition, first aid and promote healthy lifestyles.

In our society we have individuals that for whatever the reason, call it plain stupidity, find themselves with a criminal record for a single, one time non-violent criminal conviction that will follow them for life. As a result they meet with great disadvantage when it comes to employment, education, housing and even financial services. Now, let me point out that I am talking about one time offenders of crimes that do not involve any form of violence, rape, abuse against women or children, sex crimes, firearms, weapons, or explosives. It is my belief that if such an individual has served their sentence and has only a single non-violent conviction that they should not be discriminated against for a stupid mistake in their past. If we want to curb the tide of criminal repeat offenders, we must make it easier for one time non-violent offenders to reintegrate into society. The quickest way to create a repeat offender is to set them loose in public with limited employment and housing prospects. No matter what your religion, ethics or politics, I am sure that somewhere you were taught about forgiveness and compassion. Non-violent one time offenders deserve a one time second chance.

On the issue of crimes involving murder, violence, and rape I have made my position clear many times that I truly believe that we as a society must have a zero tolerance policy. I believe in capital punishment for these crimes. However, unlike the investigative and judicial process we have in place currently, the system would need to incorporate additional checks and balances to ensure that the true criminal would receive the prescribed sentence. There are many news stories of how those convicted of murder and sentenced to death should be spared because of them finding religion or becoming model citizens while incarcerated. I believe that while people can forget, only their newly found God can truly forgive such a capital act, and that individual must be prepared to take responsibility for such an irrevocable act before their God.

We in the western world take a great deal for granted. There is perhaps no place on earth where there exists such diversity of opportunity for some and struggles for daily survival for others. No matter who or where you are, you have the ability to control how the situations you encounter in your life will affect you. You cannot change the personal agendas of others or in most circumstances, the stupidity and ignorance of others. However, you can control how you react to such actions and situations. How you react, or the reaction options you have to choose from will have a direct impact on how you live from that moment on. There is a saying, "never attribute to malice what is purely an act of ignorance." There will always be people that will be smarter, dumber, richer, poorer, more beautiful and even uglier than you. You have to accept it and not take the actions of others personally. For eight long years I studied martial arts and had seen many go from white belt to black belt. Every true martial artist will tell you that the belts really mean nothing but are milestones that are earned and won as a result of hard work and dedication. In competition there are always winners and losers. Whether someone is a winner or loser is determined by strict standards and each competitor must demonstrate their skill fairly and in accordance with the rules.

However, in the real world, outside of the arts and sporting arenas, there are no winners or losers but survivors, casualties and victims. In the real world, people will use every possible loophole they can, and if that doesn't work they may boldly ignore the tenets of acceptable behavior. Survivors are those that survive such situations, casualties are those that suffer set backs and damages but still get up and regroup for another day, and then there's the victims. The victims just wallow in the hopelessness of their situation, offer opinions based on hearsay and are usually identified by the phrases "if I only" or "they/you never let me" in the brief moments when they are not competing for the underdog, done wrong by the world prize. Victims die a slow and agonizing death by their own choice. Consider who you are, and whom you really want to be. There is no one else on this earth with your skills or experience.

The only real reason people have fear is because they do not understand—they do not have enough information—are unfamiliar. It is human nature to fear things we do not understand or are unfamiliar with. Caution is an intellectually rooted emotion, fear is its pure adrenaline (sometimes evil) emotional twin. The only way to be without fear is through knowledge but this is not always possible (like trying to know the outcome of a situation with unknown human responses). Therefore, to truly strive toward fearlessness in the sense of being without fear puts one in a false sense of security. The better bet is to strive for fearlessness in the sense of going beyond fear. In this situation, you still have fear but it is only a minor emotion compared to your sense of adventure, determination and survival.

Faith is a characteristic that requires even less information than the state of fear to manifest itself. The difference between faith and fear is that with faith one emotionally believes there will be a positive outcome, where with fear the outcome is assumed to be negative or unknown. What we determine as, or the value we assign to a situation whether it is one of faith or fear is based upon our own personal belief system, life experiences (good and bad), intellect and our current situation and surroundings. Individuals are truly the sum of their faith and fear.

Contentment with oneself is the ultimate personal goal for any human being. If you are not content, inside with yourself, everything else is on a slippery slope and is subject to distraction. You cannot be at peace with yourself, fully realize your potential, love unconditionally or understand life's big picture unless you are content with you. You are the only you, you have, so your happiness and survival must always come first. Being a martyr or self-sacrificing however romantic is absolute folly. You can only throw yourself on your sword once and that's it. No one and no cause is worth it!

Not knowing coupled with general insecurity results in want. Wanting is not contentment. If you are content with yourself, you will be regardless of how the other person feels (I know this sounds harsh but it's reality) or of all the people, things and external emotions in this existence. All of our lives we are raised to be Martyrs, to be self-sacrificing for others, to accept mediocrity in the human condition to the point that it becomes automatic, self-defeating and destructive. This does not foster contentment because we are now emotionally at the whim of those around us and their self-inflicted situations, riding their roller coaster. We have forgotten that we are animals first and humans second, and therefore have lost and demonized our instinct of self-survival in exchange for self-destruction through external forces. A person's will of self-survival should be their first and primary goal, for without it, their emotional, intellectual and physical demise is prematurely imminent and they will be of no use to themselves, those they truly care about or those things that are in their manor (my collective term for what I call the personal trinity of life, responsibility and circle of influence). Once a person emotionally and intellectually understands that their self-survival is paramount, it is only then that they realize their own personal potential and limitations; and as a result truly come to "grips" with who they really are, and find contentment. So, the answer to the question of "What is the meaning of life?" is … Contentment. It's now up to you to figure the rest out.

Whenever any religion or religious applied philosophy becomes organized there is always trouble. Less learned people try to impose their interpretation of something very straightforward on those even less learned for their own misguided or contrived goals. As a result you have doctrine laden with guilt, suffering, and elitism with complex physical, intellectual and spiritual attachment!

There are always going to be sheep (the herd) and goats (leaders) in this world. People are born with inclinations, one way or the other and both have their rightful place in society, in order to make it work. As a goat, one must always be careful to discern those philosophies, solutions or concepts disguised as empowering devices that are actually the creation of other more powerful goats whose sole purpose is to keep the herd in line and maintain control. My belief on any philosophy, religion or self-help system, new or old, is to never take anything on faith or on the testimonials of others. First prove it to yourself, then use what you can and discard the rest. Don't buy into one man's or one group's concept or interpretation. The truth never set anyone free, only doubt can open the door to real freedom. The freedom of knowing and experiencing truth firsthand, not what someone else wants you to believe is truth. A child always asks, "why" in order to understand the true world as it is, because truth is more valuable than social self or acceptance.

However, as adults we seldom ask "why" because we let our ego, position and image in the herd get in the way, and accept the definition of our world according to faceless "reputable" sources. It is these very things that make slaves their own master (they bind themselves with someone else's truth); while free men answer only to themselves. Traditional slavery has always put the physical body in bondage with chains and mechanical restraints. Modern day slavery puts the body in bondage through the mind by way of misinformation, partial truth and the concept of social acceptance.

I have long held that when it comes to true evil in this realm, it is not by the hand of those that follow a god, nor those that follow a satanic path. For these individuals, although at complete opposites of the spectrum, have all one thing in common and that is a sense of self. True evil acts are committed by individuals that have no sense of self, no sense of survival and therefore have nothing to lose or gain in this world, in heaven or in hell.

So now you have my personal rant on some of the issues in our world. If I made you stop and think or consider a different angle to at least one issue or provided some point of trivia, then what I have written has not gone in vain. Even if tomorrow, you say to an associate or family member, "… that guy Ing has some really screwy opinions. I read in his book…." I know I have done my job.

The following chapters refer to incidents and cases in which I have been involved. By reading this first chapter, you now have a point of reference as to how the storyteller, me, predicates their actions under certain circumstances.

People do all forms of improbity in their anarchic pursuit of money, power and politics.

There is a dangerous practice in the Western world. Whenever society is threatened or violated, the authorities begin curtailing the rights and freedoms of their citizens and feel duty bound to bolster the ranks and firepower of uniformed officers. Technology is employed to control, monitor and track the general population in the interest of public safety. We point outward beyond our borders and reassure the masses that the threat is from without not within. The only problem is this practice does not address the original causes of the threat or violation. It is only through training and empowerment of the people already in the front line, an effective intelligence gathering methodology, redundant authenticated communication networks and an effective public safety awareness program that we can truly safeguard our community and country.

To commit murder by technology does not require an aggressor to physically end a person's life. What it really involves is collecting every single detail about that person's recent past and current activities to the point where they become a predictable non-entity. The instinct of fear is only present when we do not understand the potential of a situation or individual. Thus, they are no longer a threat or are we fearful of them because we know everything about them. We do this by tracking everything they purchase in their daily lives from bus tickets, groceries, theatre tickets, subscriptions to holiday bookings. We have the technology to track them within four feet using their mobile telephone, utilizing the GPS tracking system in their vehicles, and through the use of their security access card, all modern conveniences that most unknowingly trade their privacy for. We observe them in their daily routine via security video, access cards and who they associate with via telephone call, Internet and e-mail address records. We have retrieved their resume, credit history, driver's abstract, genealogy, birth and school records. We know their likes, dislikes, problems, triumphs and goals. They are so predictable and vulnerable to the skilled individual or organization that can piece all these traces of their daily life together that they are truly reduced to a non-entity.

Enter a world where technology is a tool of manipulation used by politicians to pass hidden agendas, by business to track individuals, by criminals to evade the law, and by terrorists as an instrument of torture and death.

This is not fiction. This is fact. This is Technology Crime. Where things happen at the speed of light, and will change the lives of every citizen.

CHAPTER 2

▼

Operation Midnight Runner:
THE ARABIAN SEA AFFAIR

*"There are more ignorant people in this world than malicious ones.
The problem is that the ignorant recognize an act of ignorance as
an act of malice. The malicious promote ignorance in order to
enslave others to unknowingly do their bidding."*

—Robert Ing

In February of 1997 I had been retained as a Special Advisor to
the Territorial Police under the auspices of a Western foreign
aid package that had been brokered between governments in
order to stabilize the region. My position entailed providing
guidance on forensic evidence recovery and technology crime to
several newly formed investigative units within the department.
Unlike other advisors before me, who were just happy to teach
in a classroom or advise from an office, I surprised my hosts by
actually going out on routine patrols and investigations. By
doing this, not only could the men and women who put their
lives on the line daily see that I wasn't just some advisor who
taught concepts from a safe distance but one who actually got in

the "trenches" with them, ducking abuse and bullets alongside them. In every assignment as an advisor, I always endeavored to earn the respect and privilege of teaching these brave men and women by advising them as an equal at their side, not from a safe distance treating them as students or even worse, subordinates. Needless to say, my application and belief in this methodology has placed me in several life threatening scenarios, not to mention political and legal fallout.

One such situation involved an operation where the undercover drug and smuggling enforcement unit of the Territorial Police were assigned a project to shut down a cross-border drug and firearms running operation. An organized gang in the prefecture was running drugs into a neighboring country, and then using the money to purchase illegal firearms and running them back into the prefecture to supply to local gangs. The atrocities of the local gangs were not for the faint of heart and included random executions, bombings and live human mutilation of victims. These atrocities were motivated by activities such as squeezing protection money from local business, loan sharking and general racketeering. Any small successful attempt to slow down or at the very least reduce the terror brought on by these gangs would be a victory given the circumstances.

My introduction as to the depth of terror that one gang was capable of came during a raid on a small home in the outskirts of the city. We had been tipped off that some gang members had taken the house by force, were holding the residents captive and attempting to set up a base of operations just west of the city. We arrived at the house just at sun up and deployed our Emergency Action Team, the equivalent to a U.S. SWAT team around the house. Despite the delusional efforts of the Captain of the Emergency Action Team to move in with as low a profile as possible; the roar of the police APVs (Armored Personnel Vehicle) engines and the aggressive para-militaristic appearance and moves of men armed to the teeth in tan BDUs (Battle Dress Uniforms) was as low profile as having a movie marquee in front of the place with the title, "Raid Today." The mentality of this high octane level testosterone show wrapped up in bravado was a clear demonstration of command and control of an unknown situation through brute force intimidation. When I was in the military we used to refer to this as FOGS (Fear Of God Syndrome), in that if you had the upper hand on your opponent you played up your position as the crazed aggressor, so that if your opponent didn't want to meet their God real soon, they had better surrender and cooperate. If the occupants of the house didn't know we were coming, they must have known at that point we had arrived. The Captain rambled some words off in the local language through a bullhorn that had a few dents and bullet holes in its trumpet. The occupants met the Captain's words with a few glances through the windows of the house, only noticeable by the movement of the loosely woven rope curtains that otherwise seemed to float behind the windows. The Captain seemed really upset that he didn't get the response he wanted, which I felt certain was an aggressive amount of gun play. You see in this part of the world, despite reforms and western aid, the bottom line was that justice was administered at either the stock or barrel end of a firearm, and some of those taken into custody would either disappear or die while awaiting trial.

The Captain gave the hand gesture for his men to tighten up the perimeter they had established around the house; that is, they moved closer to the dwelling.

Once in position, the Captain ordered that CS (tear) gas be deployed through two windows of the dwelling. CS gas is actually ortho-chlorobenzylidene malononitrile, a potentially lethal chemical that works instantaneously upon contact, causing burning eyes, coughing, breathing difficulty, stinging skin, and vomiting. Exposure amounts of CS gas must carefully be determined, particularly in closed areas, as area saturation leads to fatal suffocation. CS gas was invented in 1928 and its name bears the initials of its American inventors; Carson and Staughton. I mention this because it is a very common error that CS is assumed to be an abbreviation of its chemical name or that it is confused with OC (pepper spray) gas; Oleoresin Capsicum which is considered non-lethal.

The launch of two CS gas canister grenades was executed with as much precision as the situation would allow and slowly but surely, the occupants of the house marched single file through the front door with their hands on their heads; teary eyed, and coughing. It was obvious that these guys knew the drill and had no intention of fighting that morning. Cursory identification of these individuals indicated that they were street muscle and runners used by the gang. Quite often gang lieutenants would recruit young but poor, unschooled men from the street. For them this was the only real opportunity to escape poverty in a country with no middle class; where people were either extremely poor or extremely wealthy. As a result, once recruited and having tasted the spoils of crime they became addicted to the point where they would do anything including murder to avoid going back to the street. The story this group told were that they were brought in by truck from a neighboring village the day before and told to wait in the house for instructions. For the most part, street muscle like these guys blindly followed the orders given them without questions or morals. At the time we had no choice but to take them at face value. However, what appeared to be amiss were the hostages.

Once the gas cleared, my student forensics team entered the home, secured the area as best we could and conducted a room by room inventory and survey in search of any evidence that would help track down and identify gang leaders and their plans. As we conducted the room by room survey, I could not help but feel that something was very wrong, despite outward appearances to the contrary. Having completed the survey of the house, I recalled seeing a small clapboard utility shed at the side of the private dirt road that led to the house. I instructed one of the members of my student forensics team to conduct a survey of the shed as well. It didn't take long before the student came running up the road towards me, pale as a ghost and babbling in his native language. He grabbed my arm and literally ran dragging me along with him to the shed. He pushed me toward the shed door, while staying in my shadow, almost hiding behind my back.

The shed had no windows, but the sunlight shining through the door and between the cracks of the clapboard appeared to put rays of light across what appeared to be two bodies. The shed had a salty odor of iron. This was not a good thing, for that is the odor of blood. An odor that I had encountered many times in my life as a forensic investigator and as an emergency medical responder. I removed my flashlight from my belt, double-clicked the on button to full intensity where the bright light revealed the bodies of a woman and her child. Both woman and child were achromatic in pools of their own blood. Woman and child had been literally hacked to death with parts of their flesh actually peeled to the bone. Contrary to popular assumption, not all forensic scientists deal with cadavers and I am one of them. My forensic areas of expertise are technology crime, fingerprinting and skeletal identification. Not cadavers. As a result, we immediately radioed for the Superintendent of Public Health, a Medical Doctor who acted as an ad hoc Medical Examiner. In the interim, I had my students secure the scene until the Doctor arrived. The Doctor arrived about two hours later and under his watchful eye, photographs of the bodies and samples were taken. Later examination revealed that the victims were held down, had their vocal cords, and tendons and ligaments of their arms and legs severed by a surgical instrument while they were still alive. Thus, they could not cry for help nor move, but at the same time were fully conscious while they were bleeding to death. To make the torture all the more worse, their captors continued to peel the flesh from their bodies. This was the trademark of this gang and a warning to anyone who would get in their way. They would stop at nothing and respected no one.

During the course of three weeks, I had participated with the undercover unit in no less than six raids, arrests, searches and evidence seizures in an attempt to stem the violence. Of major concern was how information was being communicated between the runners in each country as well as to their illegal firearms merchants. Months of telephone and mail monitoring proved nothing. Likewise, computers seized during raids had minimal records and no e-mail communications of interest between suspects. If there was a way to determine how the runners passed information to each other, the good guys could not only have the incriminating evidence for a strong case but also be able to determine drop-off points, the names of others involved and even the potential list of targets to be bombed and victims slated for execution or torture. Even when suspects were arrested, they were all found to contain nothing in the way of delivery or contact information.

During each raid, when suspects were arrested all personal items on their person were inventoried and held pending their release, but in this part of the world, bail was not a common option for most arrested, and they would spend three months or more in jail before even being considered for a hearing or trial. Faced with the problem of not having any real indication of how plans were communicated between the gangs and their suppliers, I decided to examine the personal belongings of each individual runner. In all, there were about 20 different property envelopes containing the personal items recovered from the pockets of 20 individuals, men, women and children. A brief scan of the items would give the impression that they were all common items, such as wallets, currency, identification cards, credit cards and travel papers.

As a personal project and a training exercise for my evidence recovery class I was to teach the next day, I persuaded the powers that be to allow my students and I to conduct forensic examinations on a random number of the contents of the property envelopes. Besides, this was the only way that I, as an outside advisor could gain authorization to use the limited facilities of the make shift forensic laboratory that had been put together only months before my arrival. The exercise I proposed would take the form of document examination (checking for forged or altered documents), trace element residue analysis (from wallet pockets/windows), and a general UV inspection of all the selected items. The next day the exercise began and we were able to ascertain that some documents had been forged using a specific method that could only be employed by one "legitimate" business in the area. Further examination of residues in the wallets found cocaine residue of a consistency associated with a local gang operation. Needless to say, the exercise proved to provide additional leads for investigators to follow-up. However, what became obvious was that in all of the suspects' property envelopes were expired credit cards. While the question as to why anyone would carry expired credit cards was baffling, what was more baffling was that none of the suspects had any current credit cards.

A visual examination of the credit card numbers confirmed that while these were valid credit card numbers, the cards in question were counterfeit. All authentic credit card numbers must conform to an International Standard known as ISO/IEC 7812. Valid credit card numbers can be verified using what is known as the Luhn Algorithm Validation. The first step in validating a credit card number is to write it out on a piece of paper, then place a check mark over every second digit of the card number working from right to left; that is the opposite to the way you would normally read it. Then you multiply each digit you have a check mark over by 2. If the product of any number is a two digit number, say you multiplied the number 7 by 2 and arrived at 14, you just add the two digits, in this case 1 + 4 to get a single digit, 5. Once all of the second digits have been multiplied by 2 and you have reduced each product to single digits, add these together. Now add the unchecked numbers of the credit card number together. If in your addition of either the second digits products or remaining unchecked credit card numbers you arrive at a two digit number, don't reduce them to a single digit but keep them as they are. Now add the sums of these together. If the credit card number is a valid one, the total should be divisible by 10 with no remainder.

When we examined the credit card numbers in this way, we were able to determine that they were valid numbers. Of course, there are programs known as credit card number generators that are often used by the criminal and terrorist community specifically to generate valid credit card numbers for the purpose of identity theft or fraud and it shouldn't have come as a surprise that the credit card numbers in this situation would not pass the validation algorithm.

However, despite the valid card numbers, what gave the cards away as counterfeits was the fact that the major industry identifier prefix on the cards did not match the type of credit card the number was embossed on. This prefix is the very first digit of the credit card number, reading from the left. A credit card issued by a bank or financial institution will have its number start with a 4 or 5; a card issued by a petroleum company will have its number start with a 7, a 6 is issued by a merchant bank or retailer, and the prefix 3 is associated with a travel, entertainment or dining company card. In the case of the seized cards, we had bank credit card numbers embossed on travel cards and petroleum company credit card numbers embossed on bank cards. Obviously whoever created the cards had the technology but did not know its correct application.

Given the limited resources at the forensics laboratory, I attempted to run as many tests as I could on the cards to determine their worth to the runners. Interrogations by police of the suspects regarding the cards proved of little value, as all the runners would not reveal their significance for fear of death by gang leaders. Back in the lab, out of curiosity I decided to see what type of data was recorded on the magnetic strip of the credit cards. A typical credit card will have the account number, cardholders' name, card expiration date and system validation data on the strip; I had no immediate reason to expect its presence or absence. The magnetic strip on the back of a credit card has the technical capability of containing three tracks of information. However, most credit cards only utilize two tracks. Track one will contain high density formatted alpha-numeric data indicating the account number, cardholder name and card expiration date. Track two will contain low density formatted numeric only data indicating the account number and expiration date. Credit cards use two tracks to provide information compatibility to older low density format systems and current high density format systems. The amount of information that can be contained on a magnetic credit card strip will depend on a standardized encoding/decoding density protocol of either 75 or 210 BPI (Bits Per Inch). A single magnetic strip on a credit card has the capacity to hold 42 to 126 characters; the equivalent of up to one and a half typed lines of information per track. Therefore, using all three tracks, the magnetic strip on a credit card could contain up to 378 characters or four and a half typed lines of information.

Reading the information on the magnetic strip of the credit card was far beyond the limited capabilities of the forensics lab. While I must say that the comradeship and association I had with the front line men and women with whom I was to train will be valued for years to come, this was not the case when it came to the Command levels of the Territorial Police. To them, I and others who were brought in as advisors were forced upon them by a Western power and their acceptance of such a program was only done because it came as a political aid package with other more desirable benefits. As well, many Police Commanders openly discounted many "western ways" and treated forensic science, let alone technology in investigation as a novelty. Thus the limited capability forensic laboratory.

I knew that if I were to retrieve any evidence from the magnetic strip of the credit cards, if there was any to retrieve, it would have to be with their blessing. In order to obtain permission to do this, I proposed that my next workshop with my students would deal with credit card fraud. At first, the Commanders made light of the issue and debated the value of such an activity but I was able to convince them that this was a major concern of western business and tourist interests and as a result would make them look good politically if they had such training. They, under the pressure of one of my local political contacts, gave their permission. For good measure, I obtained permission to use some of the credit cards obtained from the runners as exemplars in our study. The reason for me not being direct about specifically examining the cards further was due to commands inability to understand the value of technical evidence and the fact that I had been informed that within command a gang sympathizer/informant had been closely monitoring what was being done with the seized items. I knew that if I showed my hand too early and ruffled feathers too much that it could cost me my life. What I also did not tell command was that my students and I would be taking the credit cards to the hotel I was staying at to conduct the class. Out of all the places in the city, I knew that my American hotel was the safest bet for access to a credit card stripe reader.

The next day, some 20 junior police officers and I showed up at the front desk of my hotel. It was quite a sight ... almost looked like a raid. But I did this on purpose. The manager came out and after a persuasive conversation supported with a generous tip in U.S. dollars, I was allowed access to one of the three credit card readers in the hotel. Under the watchful eye of the manager and my students, I hooked up my laptop, accessed the Internet and was able to download a credit card data reading program and reader driver program. I then hooked up the reader to my serial port, rebooted my laptop and we were in business. My students soon learned the value of not knowing everything about everything but knowing where to find something when you need it. Within the hour, my students and I recovered a surprising amount of coded data from each card. Every step of the way, students took notes and by the time the last card was read, they were well versed in data recovery from a credit card.

The information retrieved on the card was coded and could have proved a challenge. However, regardless of the extreme wealth enjoyed by the political and social elite, the general population lived in squalor, which meant at best the country was sandwiched between a third and second world country. While the business elite, government and those who could afford them used computers, their use was easily five years behind the west. The country's criminal element borrowed the technology of others on a limited basis to assist in their crimes, much like the placing of data on the strip of a credit card; something credit card fraudsters in the U.S. perfected and bragged of on the Internet. Therefore, looking at the pattern of the code, my intuition and experience led me to believe that the coding scheme used was a simple, non-technical one borrowed from somewhere else. By all appearances, the coding took the form of a substitution code. That is, where one character is represented by another. My students and I would try to break the code the next day, yet another daylong workshop with a new subject—codes and ciphers.

The easiest way to crack a substitution code or cipher is to use what is known as the Entropic Attack Methodology. The Entropic Attack Methodology analyzes the way a pattern of the substituted characters appear and the frequency of the pattern in order to decode the message. Of course, the larger the coded message the shorter time it will take to break because more patterns can be observed and analyzed. However, on a typical credit card stripe there are only two tracks of information recorded with only a few having a seldom used third track. In the case of our credit cards, tracks 1 and 2 contained data to full capacity, a bonus for our side. We tried all the conventional substitution code patterns from numerology to letter/number combinations on a telephone. It was late in the afternoon when we hit pay dirt and cracked the code using a substitution code pattern known as the Red Cross Code, which was used in Africa by relief workers in the 1970's and 1980's. The Red Cross Code was not an official code of the Red Cross but rather one based on one that is allegedly attributed to Julius Caesar and is known as the Caesar Cipher. According to historical accounts, Julius Caesar used substitution ciphers to communicate with his lieutenants. The variation of the Caesar Cipher we found could be decoded based on the keys listed below, where every character to the left of the equal sign corresponded to the coded character to the right of the equal sign.

A=C, B=D, C=E, D=F, E=G, F=H, G=I, H=J, I=K,
J=L, K=M, L=N, M=O, N=P, O=Q, P=R, Q=S, R=T,
S=U, T=V, U=W, V=X, W=Y, X=Z, Y=A, Z=B
1=3, 2=4, 3=5, 4=6, 5=7, 6=8, 7=9, 8=0, 9=1, 0=2

Having decoded the data in the tracks, we found ourselves looking at what appeared to be some form of reference numbers or passwords.

The data was alpha-numeric with set patterns and groups. An example of the data looked like this:

09060C2/0425   08661A2/0501   09264D2/0607   09064B2/0710

We continued to work into the night, relentlessly trying to associate these alpha-numeric patterns with something meaningful. Some students stayed because their curiosity had been piqued, while others stayed because to call it a day would embarrass them in front of their peers. Whatever their motives, we all worked together as a team and when we got to a point where logic and science seemed to fail us, we skunk tanked theories and opinions to fuel our search for new lines of investigative points of departure.

It was about 0300 in the morning when a student came up with the idea that the codes might be geocodes. A geocode is a detailed map reference that is used to indicate specific coordinates for a given location. We immediately began pulling out all of the map books and charts we could find in order to identify, if these alpha-numeric identifiers referenced the geocode positions in any of the maps and charts we had on hand. After a few more hours of comparing and cross-referencing the codes, we realized that the first seven digits represented locations on outdated Territorial Police maps. We validated our findings as several geocode references represented gang hideouts, drop-offs and rendezvous points where police raids had been successfully executed. Further analysis of the remaining four digits after the slash mark indicated that these numbers represented dates when specific events were scheduled to occur, such as a drop-off, rendezvous or even worse, an attack. For me, that moment was really what the science of Forensic Intelligence was all about. We had the technology and skills to acquire and analyze the information in order to identify and validate past criminal acts and to identify potential crime risk.

Once the code was cracked, the challenge was to establish surveillance operations at the locations we identified and execute intervention at the appropriate moment. Given that access to even decommissioned police maps and charts was restricted, this underscored the theory that someone within the Territorial Police was assisting the gang by providing operational methodology support. I had to tread lightly in presenting our findings and recommendations to command. While I had suspected some individuals at the command level of being in league with gang leaders, I could not substantiate this. Nor did I know who to really trust. A mistake or error in judgment on my part could cost the lives of some of my students and myself if it came to light that we had the intelligence required for an effective interdiction operation against the terror of this gang.

I could do nothing, after all, many looked upon me and my forensic advisor-instructor role as nothing more than a novelty to be entertained for a few months that would culminate with me boarding an aircraft headed back home never to be seen again. Unfortunately, many advisors brought in under foreign aid packages followed this regimen, just happy to put yet another "hollow" accolade on their resume. They just marked time during their call out; being paraded for every possible photo opportunity with powerful locals. I simply could not do this after seeing the terror on the ground firsthand. I also owed a great deal to the men and women of my student forensics team and was not going to discount the hard work and passion they put in to help track down these terrorists.

The next day I arranged to have lunch at the Consulate with the U.S. Diplomatic Affairs Officer (DAO) and political liaison. We met at the staff club room where black bow-tied waiters dressed in white shirts and jackets with black pants pressed to the point where the press line alone could cut a baguette, performed an unhurried relay between the tables. The dark wood paneled wall décor, the dark green upholstery, dark wood furniture and polished brass accents with a 14 karat gold luster seemed completely surreal compared to the world on the other side of the walls.

After exchanging pleasantries and the usual small talk, lunch was almost over. At that point I decided to play my hand. I related details of my teams' investigation and findings. I also intimated the possible fatal consequences for my team members and myself if this information got into the wrong hands or was acted upon incorrectly. The two politicos looked at each other with that usual rehearsed look of disbelief. You know, the look that a politician will give on live television when they deny everything, admit nothing and try to pacify the public by setting up a committee of inquiry to blame someone else. This was the look. They knew what was going on. I knew before I had even asked to see them that they knew about the internal corruption but as long as it wasn't a major threat to the political dynamos at home and didn't interfere with the ultimate agenda of containment of the area, the situation was deemed tolerable.

I had to really do a political sell to get the outcome I figured was the only way to break up the terror inflicted on the ground by these gangs and possibly save some lives in the bargain. I pitched my persuasive proposal with the angle how it would be good media for the aid effort back home, if we were actually able to be identified as having made real inroads on rounding up terrorists. You see, the public back home was getting tired of supporting and sending people overseas for situations that they could not justify as posing a threat to their own personal lifestyle. The nation's leader was falling in popularity polls with an impending scandal inquiry and a general dissent from the opposition. I argued that this would take some media pressure off of these issues and provide a positive spin on the administration. The politicos bought into it, but were concerned about the gang sympathizers within the Territorial Police and how we could successfully pull off a multiple surveillance and raid operation without their blessing.

As part of the aid package, a handful of western allies had provided military advisors and small training units as part of a multi-national force within the Territory. This force although sent primarily to train the nationals, also provided interdiction support under the watchful eye of the Territorial Police. My recommendation was to deploy these forces within very close proximity to the target areas my team identified. Then, at the first sign of activity, call in the locals, execute engagement and secure these areas. That is, get the bad guys. By the time the dust would settle, it would be too late to tip off the bad guys. The plan called for the multi-national teams to be assigned training missions or civilian/humanitarian aid projects within proximity of the target areas or where they would have to travel several times a day through the target areas. After about another hour of persuasion and frustration, I had left with an agreement that they would make the call to the Executive Office and get approval.

Back at the lab my students and I were able to perform further analysis on the remaining credit cards, and were able to establish a pattern on how the drop offs were rotated based on the sequence of when each runner had been arrested. In order to establish the patterns and possibilities we used one of my favorite analytical and note taking tools known as a mind map. The art and science of mind mapping was developed by Tony and Barry Buzan, and I had stumbled across it years ago while working in the United Kingdom. Mind mapping starts with a single concept or idea and then enables you to literally branch that concept into allied concepts with their own sub-concepts. Mind mapping is a great deal easier to use and understand than I can explain it, and I really can't do it justice here. I have used mind mapping to take notes and as an analytical investigative aid for years and encourage anyone who hates taking notes or is interested in a simple analytical tool to do some research on Tony Buzan, Barry Buzan and Mind Maps. The use of mind mapping as an integral part of my professional life actually had colleagues at one of my places of employ consider me to be some kind of mad scientist but I think they were just frustrated because it wasn't part of the status quo. In any case, my Renaissance Art Leather Journal also known as my mind map book is a regular investigative accessory I won't leave home without.

The next day I received a call from the Commander of the multi-national force on the ground. His call was brief and told me to meet him at his office at 1500 hours that day. This was a good sign, I knew that he had received his orders and just wanted my input for the pre-briefing that would follow with his officers. The multi-national force command headquarters was housed in an old dilapidated three story brick brownstone apartment building. The building had been evacuated over three years ago after part of it fell victim to a suicide bomber in a two and half ton truck determined to ram the building. The building built around the 1940's proved that it could withstand the attack and while cosmetically looked like a disaster, the structure was intact. The Commander's office was on the third floor, which meant a walk up six sets of stairs while trying to avoid stepping on the plaster, paint chips and dead insects that littered the stairs. An elevator never existed in this type of building and given the circumstances and my personal experience; if you value your life, the last thing you want to do is to get trapped in an elevator due to a power outage caused by a firefight or bombing. As well, you just never know who will be on the other side of those elevator doors when they open up; you could very well end up on the wrong end of a weapon. Despite the heat and humidity in the stairwells, the stairs were definitely a healthy option.

Having arrived at the third floor, I made my way down the straight and narrow mint green painted corridor to the Commander's office. I walked through the open door where I was greeted by a Master Warrant Officer. Before I could say anything, the MWO asked are you, "Ing"? I responded, "yes, Warrant." "Wait here Sir," he barked. He walked through a door to his left which was probably someone's bedroom at one point, noticeable by the tell tale glimpse I got of the peach color paint on the wall before the door closed behind him. The MWO came out and said the Commander will see you now, as he escorted me into a near empty peach room with only a desk overflowing with papers on it and four wooden chairs around it, all in the center of the room. Standing off in the corner, sizing me up was the Commander. The Commander said, "Captain, I know what you have been up to and what you are trying to pull off here." "I have been advised to work with you on this, but it is not my intention to unnecessarily compromise any of my men." From the Commander's first words I knew that between the lines, he wanted to make it clear that there was no way that he was going to let any wet behind the ears subordinate (me) tell him how to run his shop.

It was never my intention to impose on, or even consider such a thing. One of the greatest falsehoods we are told all through life is that everyone is created equal and that we as individuals can accomplish anything. This is not true and many good men and women have failed or even worse have died buying into this lie. As individuals, part of our personal growth and maturing process requires that we learn empirically that every person has their own set of positive and negative abilities, situation and views. Therefore, we are not equal and what is easy for one person to achieve may be the unachievable for another. We must know our own limitations, or in essence "the box" that we are stuck in. Once we know our limitations and the reality that we can never go beyond "the box" it is only then that we can focus ourselves on being the very best in "the box" and if we so desire, achieve greatness in our own right. There will be many occasions when we do need skills and experience beyond our limitations in order to create an opportunity where we can achieve our objective. A benefit of knowing yourself and limitations enables you to confidently seek out other individuals with skills and abilities that you do not possess in order to achieve your goals. This must always be a reciprocal relationship; where you also offer your skills and abilities in a mutually beneficial situation for others to achieve their goals.

My strength and ability would never match the experience, skill and insight required to successfully execute this mission and I made this clear to the Commander. In the three hours that followed, I briefed the Commander on the situation, identified the mission objective, addressed exactly what I was expecting from him and his men and reaffirmed his role in the planning, deployment and execution on the ground. He accepted the task, albeit cautiously, but in the time that we spent together, we both realized a greater respect of each other's role.

The operation entailed two weeks of surveillance work on no less than six key locations. Multi-national forces in place alongside undercover officers would maintain surveillance on the drop off points and track the participants to gang lieutenants and organizers. The mission posed several challenges for everyone involved from trying to blend in and not arousing undue attention to the extreme heat in the day. Despite the fact that we knew what day the rendezvous at each location would take place, it was imperative that our surveillance teams got settled in days in advance, so that the locals and even the men would become part of the scenery.

The toughest thing about surveillance work is trying to stay alert and focused while maintaining a low profile. Generally a surveillance operative will be at his or her best within the first four hours of deployment. For every hour up to four hours an operative keeps watch, their powers of observation and alertness will decline by about 10% for each hour that nothing happens. At the four hour point, they are only functioning at 60% and for every hour after that, there is a steady decline of alertness, averaging 12% per hour. At the end of an 8 hour shift with nothing happening, the operative's level of focus and alertness may only be at 12% efficiency. Even at an efficiency level of 40%, small nuances such as noticing an individual in a group of people wearing a vest on a public street with tell-tale signs of explosives sewn into the lining may easily go unnoticed. In a surveillance operation in hostile territory it is critical that each member of the team work in all positions on a rotational basis throughout the 8 hour duty tour. A team member may start at the watch position for the first two hours, then move on to a back-up position for the next two hours, an intercept position for the next two hours and then take a point position for the last two hours of the tour. This keeps the team fresh and focused, ready to observe and act upon any situation that may arise.

With our teams in place, we watched and waited. In the two weeks that followed our deployment, our teams were able to follow other gang members from the locations we had identified to other hideouts and widen our net. Unfortunately, the majority of the raids we executed culminated in firefights where gang members and our teams engaged them in what only could be considered as intense exchanges of bullets.

One raid incident that I will never forget occurred when a gang held up in a small abandoned store, after exchanging weapons fire for about 15 minutes with our teams decided to surrender. They threw their weapons onto the street and waved rags through the already broken windows. Then, following the bull-horned instructions of one of our team's Lieutenants began to slowly march single file out the front door of the shop with their hands placed behind their head and, on command, kneeled on the curb, still with their hands behind their heads, in a line parallel to the bullet ridden storefront. I recall seeing what looked like a small man, about 4' 11", the shortest of the gang members come out, but he did not stop to kneel. He continued walking towards our position with hands on his head despite orders to stop and kneel down. As he got closer, I noticed that he had clenched in his left fist some object that he was holding next to his head. His unbuttoned shirt seemed to lift to the right, either by the wind or his walking, it revealed something taped to his side that looked like a field dressing or make shift bandage.

I had seen this all before, in a war zone. I quickly raised my sidearm and was about to pull the trigger of my pistol to shoot him in the left arm. However, a sharpshooter also realized what I had seen and fired a single shot just as I was to pull the trigger. As the sound of the single weapon echoed, the short man fell back to the ground, and remained motionless. The man had been stopped in a matter of not more than two seconds. Moments after the scene was secured, I walked up to the man, who was very still. The sharpshooter put a bullet right through the head of this person, killing him instantly as the round entered and exited the skull. Upon closer examination, my instinct was correct; the gang member had an explosive device taped to his side and he had been holding some kind of trigger in his hand while walking towards us. His mission was clear, to kill as many of our team as possible and sacrifice himself in the process. The explosives team in securing the scene had already removed the detonator, so all was safe. However, upon taking an even closer look at this victim, looking beyond the ragged clothing and dirty, unwashed face and hair, I realized that this was a small girl of not more than 11 years old.

The raids were executed at all the locations and we were able to take into custody a total of 126 gang members and seize large quantities of cash, drugs and weapons. Gang casualties numbered 33 wounded and 15 dead. Our teams suffered 4 casualties and 1 dead, only because we had the benefit of surprise, body armor and a planned methodology. Contact lists naming local political sympathizers and information pertaining to police activities had been also recovered, which pointed to Command Officers in the Territorial Police who would have been the only persons privy to that specific information. Immediate raids and arrests were made at the homes and offices of these individuals without incident.

About one week after the final raid I was summoned to a meeting at the consulate with the Diplomatic Affairs Officer. We exchanged a great deal of small talk for about 2 hours and then he got to the real reason why he wanted to see me. He handed me a sealed tyvek envelope from the Department of Foreign Affairs. In addition to the usual address information, it had been rubber stamped on the back and front, "To Be Opened By Addressee Only" and its flap had been sealed with tamper proof security tape. As I opened the envelope, I removed another smaller tyvek envelope with a yellow "Confidential" label with my name typed on it, and the required tamper proof security tape on the flap. Having opened the second envelope, I found a letter thanking me for my services in helping fulfill my government's aid commitment to the region and my orders recalling me back home. My itinerary for recall was to be executed within 48 hours and left very little time for long goodbyes.

Through the dedication and efforts of the student forensic team who cracked the credit card code, and Multi-National Force members and local police field officers who risked their lives to execute the raids; this violent gang had been destroyed after five long years of a reign of terror. The ousted and arrested Police Command Officers mysteriously disappeared while in holding cells prior to their trials and it is believed that they were executed.

CHAPTER 3

▼

Operation Mysteron:
THE EXECUTIVE AIR
AFFAIR

*"Freedom is only possible at the compromise of others. The ability of
one to compromise is directly proportional to their survival."*

—Robert Ing

It was 2300 hours, and the sleek Cessna Citation jet touched
down right on time at the Metropolitan International Airport
private terminal. It had rained most of the afternoon and into
the evening as the tarmac glistened with the reflection of airport
marker lights. Looking out from the private terminal and across
the runways and taxiways you could see the three commercial
terminals with their spotlights illuminating the Airbuses and
Boeing 777 jets all docked in close quarters around the
terminals like bees around a hive in the distance. The
commercial terminals made the private terminal look more like
a small bus terminal by comparison. It could have easily been a
bus terminal that had been converted into an air terminal. From

the large glass windows in the private terminal waiting area, I watched as the Cessna Citation taxied so that it would stop parallel to the terminal window. The spotlights of the airfield reflected off of the semi-wet white fuselage with its robin egg blue flashing and gold accents as the aircraft gently stopped in front of the terminal. This would be the beginning of what I thought was going to be another uneventful assignment.

The Cessna Citation was a private corporate jet that shuttled the President and CEO of RKR Corporation, an international telecommunications company and one of America's Top 100 corporations. My assignment, for the past several months was whenever the aircraft arrived in the city, I was to ensure that it was secured until takeoff. Secured in this sense of the assignment meant that my employers were concerned about authorized and unauthorized individuals placing electronic surveillance or explosive devices on the aircraft, or even worse sabotaging the avionics of the craft. RKR and my employers had reason to be concerned, particularly because some areas of RKR's product and service portfolio placed it as a defense and intelligence contractor to what was considered U.S. friendly nations. However, as history has shown many times, foreign policy in concert with paranoia is a fickle thing, and often in the second or third world, today's allies have the potential of being tomorrow's enemies. One of the worst things that can happen to a second or third world nation that depends on western foreign aid, is to buy a truckload of military or spy hardware and later fall out of favor, be blacklisted and have almost no one willing to sell them spare parts during the height of civil unrest or alleged military threat from a neighboring country.

It doesn't seem long ago that in the 1980's, the selling of an Atari video game system to an Eastern European nation was forbidden under American law for fear that the computer chip in the game could be removed and utilized in the design of a nuclear missile weapons guidance system. In the post 2001 world, the selling of U.S. manufactured or made for U.S. market computers and microprocessor based electronics outside the country is forbidden, in the interest of U.S. national security. This is enforced even to allies such as Canada whose troops can be found in an often dangerous support role alongside their U.S. military counterparts in the world's trouble spots. Yes, Canadians cannot order a Dell Computer from the U.S.! Rather, they must go through a Canadian call center, typically routed to a second world nation, that orders a made for non-U.S. market product. Of course the real irony is that most, if not all of today's sophisticated electronic devices, even those used in military applications have genealogical ties either by manufacture or assembly to some non-U.S. source with much more relaxed protocols for acquisition.

It is also no secret that if you want to convince a foreign government to accept your government's foreign policy, you contain it rather than send in the troops. Containment is done through sanctions. Sanctions, particularly of food and medicines, have the potential of killing more foreign nationals than sending in troops. If you want to ground a squadron of high tech jet fighters or disable an early warning defense system, you don't have to send in the troops, just put a trade embargo on simple components such as the special fuses or indicator LEDs (Light Emitting Diodes) used in these devices and just wait it out. Without replacements, the computers on these systems shut down and the people of the opposing forces, who favor your foreign policy, will seize power. While involved in another project overseas, I had witnessed the bombing of a small village, while six military jet fighters remained grounded and later fell victim to the bombing. When I asked why the jets were not scrambled to protect the village and airfield, the Commander replied that due to embargos, there were no parts to keep the aircraft flying.

On the other hand, if you must stabilize a region, you would send in troops in order to secure command and control of foreign resources and assets to ensure the stability of your trading partner's ability to fulfill the needs of your nation. Oil, gold, diamonds and potentially hostile governments (with resources/assets your country needs) are still at the top of the list for sending in troops to stabilize regions. Another, recent addition to this list of resources is cheap labor. By stabilizing a country that has a cheap labor force, your country's corporations can job out work to a favored foreign nation without having to go the route of costly immigration or security concerns, while increasing profits. Almost everyone wins, except for the workers on both sides of the ocean.

Out of all the assignments I have had, this one had to be the least planned. No pre-briefing, no briefing files. I never knew when the aircraft would arrive until I would receive a telephone call, typically six hours before touchdown. Then there was staying with the aircraft. I never knew when the aircraft was to takeoff. While I am sure someone knew, most of this information was on a need to know basis and the powers that be decided that I never needed to know. I can recall the time that I had spent 49 hours stuck onboard, just babysitting that winged boardroom.

This time just seemed like any other. Watch the ramp rats (ground maintenance staff) run the stairway up to the plane, smile and nod as the EA (executive assistant), clerical support staff, bodyguards and then the President himself deplaned. Pilot, Co-Pilot, and Safety Officer (sometimes referred to as the EXO or Executive Officer) would then leave the craft, handing her over to my care. As a kid in elementary school, I used to dream about flying such a jet and I can recall staying an extra half hour after school in Mr. Brownsberger's classroom each week to fly the Cessna 170 flight simulator that Mr. B had meticulously built literally from scratch. All it really was, was a neatly cut-out wood control panel with a yoke (that's pilot jargon for a steering wheel) made out of dowel. The panel had the instruments meticulously reproduced on construction paper appliqués. I often thought about this every time I entered the cockpits of the many aircraft I would later find myself securing as well as the times I had piloted rotorcraft. It was because of the seed that Mr. B implanted in my head, back in the days of Grades 3 and 4 that motivated me to attend pilot ground school, pursue an interest in flying, skydiving and direct my academic and professional development in science.

Nostalgia aside, I unpacked my portable particle trace detector and began my sweep of the aircraft exterior, specifically the landing gear, baggage compartment, service compartments and lower fuselage for traces of explosives. Particulate detection of specific explosive materials such as TNT, dynamite, PETN, Semtex, EGDN, DMNB, RDX (C-4), nitroglycerine (NG) and Ammonium Nitrate were on the menu of items I was always looking for, but never hoping to find. Fortunately, there is an established methodology for doing an exterior sweep of an aircraft this size and I managed to process the aircraft exterior within 1 hour with nothing found. Next came the interior. Same sweep for explosive materials but of course, many more places to check that would see me spend just under 2 hours on the interior, fortunately with nothing found. When you go beyond a 100 sweeps throughout your career and find nothing, it is very easy to get into a mindset you will never find anything and that the whole process is just to say you have done it and leave someone, somewhere with a warm feeling of being secure. I have always tried not to think of it this way, but the idea is always buried in the back of your mind somewhere. If anyone who does this for a living tells you otherwise, I would suspect they are trying to impress you on some superficial level.

It is general operating procedure to always do an explosives sweep first, followed by an electronic surveillance and control device (ESCD) sweep. The primary reason for this, is particle trace detectors are passive devices in that they simply vacuum in the air in a specific area, like a human nose to detect an explosive component. An ESCD device actually emits an extremely low power electronic radio signal known as an Intermediate Frequency (IF) signal whenever it is used. If an explosive device were onboard that happened to use a radio frequency detonator, switching an ESCD device on could prematurely trigger an explosion. This is the best reason to check for explosive devices first.

The ESCD sweep involved checking the aircraft for hidden transmitters, receivers or a combination of these two devices known as a transceiver. Concealed transmitters can be used to gather audio and video of closed door meetings and track the location of individuals. A hidden receiver could be used to remotely control or trigger other devices onboard the aircraft at anytime. A hidden transceiver planted on the aircraft could have the potential of controlling the aircraft or damaging it. In short, these devices posed a threat.

The ESCD sweep took just under an hour to complete. Everything checked out fine and now it was time for me to pack my gear away and just stay with the aircraft until the crew and passengers all arrived. Needless to say this could be within the next hour or next 48 hours. As was standard procedure, I activated two computer radio frequency scanners (CRFS) that would alert me to any form of radio transmission that might occur onboard the aircraft for the time I would be on duty or until the aircraft was ready to take-off. If I detected such a transmission, my job was to identify it, find its source, disable and retrieve the device and report it. The identification part was fairly easy as upon activation of a transmission, my CRFS would display the frequency, the mode, digitally record a sample of the signal (audio, video or data) and would access the U.S. Federal Communications Commission and Industry Canada frequency registration database to determine who allegedly owned the device. In intelligence circles, the rule of thumb to determine the ownership of a surveillance transmitter can be done by knowing its frequency and transmission mode.

Government devices have specific reserved frequencies and operate in Spread Spectrum FM mode with digital scrambling, whereas the devices sold to the public and private investigative community from retail and mail order outlets operate on what are known as commercial low power unit (LPU) frequencies in AM or FM modes with no form of scrambling and do not utilize spread spectrum technology. A mode is like AM radio vs. FM radio. Scrambling is a system used to scramble the information being transmitted so that it can only be unscrambled by someone who has the appropriate equipment. Spread spectrum means that the information, in this case voice or voice and video are sent (spread) over the entire channel which greatly reduces interference and makes it even more difficult for someone with an ordinary "consumer" brand radio or television to receive the signal. In the old spy movies, the hero would know someone had bugged his apartment because he accidentally heard his voice on the stereo or was able to watch himself on his own television set. While this may still be the case with some over the counter retail or mail order surveillance devices, I can assure you those used by domestic and foreign government agencies use digital scrambling and at best you might notice some extra static or a dead spot on your radio dial or on a television channel but you may never know if it's really static or "big brother." Just by knowing the frequency of the device and its transmission mode, a trained operative can tell you if it belongs to a federal, or state agency, foreign government, or if it was just picked up at a local electronics retail outlet.

It is also interesting to note that in 2005, the reported sales of commercial off the shelf (COTS) surveillance devices in North America was approximately 2.7 million, with 42% of these being government purchases. While 37% of all telephone taps are conducted by law enforcement (police agencies). As well, with the appearance of illusionary federal government cost cutting measures up to the year 2007 many low level security services are now contracted out to the private sector. What this really means is that it will actually cost the taxpayer more, but as this increased expense comes out of a different budget, politicians and bureaucrats can boast how they reduced public safety spending without loss of service. A more sinister concern is when it comes to personal rights, freedoms and privacy; citizens are protected in their dealings with the government under the Constitution in the United States and the Charter of

Rights in Canada. It is accepted that these documents are applicable to the dealings a citizen would have between them and their government. However, with the privatization of many security, intelligence, investigative and law enforcement functions traditionally performed by government; government agencies that were restricted in their methodology when dealing with the public are hiring private companies to do the same function but the major difference is that the private entity is not legally subject to the same stringent methodology or accountability model. Therefore, a non-government entity providing a service on behalf of government may exercise a greater latitude in the performance of its duties at the expense of a citizen's rights and privacy.

My total time with the aircraft at this point was just over twelve hours. However, the time had passed quite quickly as in addition to all of the sweeps I made of the craft, I started my reports detailing all of the security procedures I performed, known collectively as Counter-Measures Testing and Verification. As I completed my final report, I noticed the ramp rats checking the electrical system of the aircraft and positioning service vehicles next to the craft. This was a clear indicator that they were getting this bird ready for departure and that the crew, the President and his entourage would no doubt arrive within 90 minutes. My MARCO unit indicated that I had received an encrypted message. The MARCO was a wireless militarized, second generation PDA manufactured by Motorola based on the Apple Newton but as large as a hardcover desk version of the Oxford Dictionary with an onboard 30 MB flash card memory. Compare that to the size of today's personal organizers or palmtop computers!

After running MARCO's installed Digital Encryption Standard (DES) and authentication software to decode the message, my orders were to remain with the aircraft and accompany the President back to his next destination. After securing the aircraft at that location, I would then be flown back on one of my employers' agency aircraft. To be honest, I looked forward to the flight back even though it would be at least another day and a half away, because I knew then, that I would really be able to relax and stand down. Although this assignment had a strict methodology and execution, it was the type of situation that even if you were not performing a specific task, you had to be alert and vigilant even while on the sidelines. If you were onboard the aircraft, you were on and you were live. If an incident occurred no matter how big or small, you only had one chance to get it right. Getting it right could mean the difference between life and death. There was absolutely no room for second guessing during a crisis.

Just like clock work, the three flight crew members; Captain, Co-Pilot and Executive Officer arrived and made their way to the cockpit for their preflight inspection. Moments later the dark blue SUV and two dark blue sedans arrived with their magnetic tear-drop shaped flashing halogen lights awkwardly positioned on the vehicle roofs breaking the otherwise surreal two dimensional scenery. The bodyguards, clerical support staff, the President's Executive Assistant and finally the President arrived and boarded the aircraft. The Security Chief gave me a reassuring nod as he passed the seat I had made myself home in, since I boarded the aircraft hours ago. I had worked with him; John, many times before, providing technical security support not just for this President but his predecessor and also for Foreign Trade Representatives. John was a 14 year

U.S. Special Forces (Green Beret) veteran whose demeanor and professionalism always gave the impression that he was a rough and tumble kind of guy that most people avoided. I knew better. He was really a gentle grizzly bear of a man, with a kind heart and the type of man you knew you could depend on to cover your back. On overseas assignments, we covered each other's backsides in many situations.

Once everyone was boarded and settled in, the usual fasten seat belt sign came on, and safety announcements were made by the Captain. The aircraft seemed to drag itself from taxiway to runway, where we held for a few moments pending clearance to take off from the tower.

As the aircraft ascended, I relaxed in my seat and got ready to catch a nap. I took a brief glance out of the window to see the sun rise as it glistened on the dull aluminum wing surface. The visibility was unlimited and you could see for miles. We leveled off at about 7000 feet and I felt myself dozing off. I must have been asleep for not more than 10 minutes, when the Executive Officer came over to me and poked me a few times to wake me. Surprised to see him, he said to me, look out your window and then you better come with me. I looked out the window and there appeared to be an aircraft of some sort, a big aircraft off the starboard (right) wing. I looked at the EXO and followed him through the aircraft towards the cockpit.

Unlike other standard executive commercial aircraft, the bird I was on was different in that it carried the chief of a major government defense contractor. It was equipped with defensive airborne security systems and warranted a Shadow Escort. A Shadow Escort consists of two low profile security escort aircraft, typically one in the front and one in the rear at different altitudes to the protected aircraft but within visual range. The

Shadow Escort takes off from a separate airport or runway after the protected aircraft is airborne in order not to draw undue attention. I figured what I had seen from my window was one of these Escorts trying to catch up and that I probably left a cable or something behind in the cockpit area when doing my sweep for explosives or transmitters.

As I walked along the aisle, I couldn't help but notice John with a serious but frustrated look on his face trying to get a comm link (radio communication link) active on an attaché case digital terminal. I thought this rather odd, as comms would ordinarily be routed through the onboard aircraft system.

Having arrived at the cabin door, the EXO inserted his access card in the reader and entered his code on the keypad to gain entry to the cockpit. The moment I came through the cabin door, the Captain said, "Protocol says I have to advise you of possible technical security issues. See that thing out there, on the starboard? Ever since it appeared we have lost comms (communications) and navigation is offline. It's flying literally alongside, about 6 miles out, matching our speed and it's about 2000 feet above our altitude. Shadow escort will not reach us for another nine minutes. If you know anything, you better tell me now."

I looked at the Captain, and advised him that I was not aware of the unidentified craft and that I had not detected any tracking or remote control devices onboard. I then asked, "How long has it been there and did you run it through ADVIS?"

ADVIS (Airborne Digital Video Imaging Security) is a system of two computer guided Pan Tilt Zoom (PTZ) digital cameras mounted one on the forecastle (lower front) of the fuselage and one on the aft quarter deck (upper rear) of the fuselage. The system is activated by radar to target an aircraft within 12 miles range and if visibility permits to identify the aircraft by profile and zoom in on the aircraft registration where a computer will automatically match the craft against a military/ commercial database of craft type and registration. Almost all aircraft have an onboard transponder that will automatically transmit an identification code indicating their registration and aircraft type. However, this system provides additional security by verifying the identity of the craft and recording it on digital video that, if communications links are active, can be transmitted live to a designated ground monitoring station.

The Captain responded, "ADVIS has it on video but there's no detectable registration markings, commercial or military. This thing is not in the database. ADVIS calculates it to be about 269 feet in diameter. There's no transponder ID. It's been matching our direction of travel for the past four minutes."

My immediate, gut question in response was, "Have you advised the President?" The Captain responded, "Security and the President's EA have been advised and we have executed AECM protocol. The President is taking a nap. However, once we can authenticate the risk level, we'll have to advise him."

AECM (Airborne Electronic Counter-Measures) protocol is an in-flight aircraft security protocol that involves the activation of electronic and physical systems to defend against an external attack from the air or ground that would target the aircraft.

As I looked out the cockpit window, I could see the grayish green smooth object with what appeared to be a streak coming out of it, similar to a contrail (condensation vapor trail). It looked solid with no sign of windows or markings.

Then, suddenly the grayish green object seemed to abruptly go into a curved trajectory from the starboard (right) side of our aircraft across the fore (front), where it became clear that this object was a disc of some sort and then it disappeared in a flash of light leaving only a contrail. Upon the moment it disappeared, indicator lights flashed and a buzzer sounded in the cockpit. The Captain turned and said, "Navigation and comms are back online." Just as he said that, the Co-Pilot seemed to spring into action feverishly toggling switches, twisting knobs and reviewing instrument readings.

We all looked at each other, not knowing what it was that we had seen, or why all communications systems shut down and then came back on as if someone turned on the power when the unidentified craft disappeared. As with protocol, the Pilot notified the nearest tower and filed a report with the aviation administration. Everyone on-board ended up filing their reports verbally and electronically with their respective agencies or supervisors. The remaining 4 hours in the air was tense but uneventful. For most of the trip, no one discussed what they had seen after the sighting. We were professionals, and silence was part of our trade. We all expected when we would touch down that we would be debriefed on this incident by our respective superiors. In my mind I couldn't help but wonder what exactly it was I had seen and what could disable the onboard communications except for a military aircraft of some form.

The touchdown was routine until we taxied up to the terminal. Outside of my window I spotted three black sedans with military license plates over and above the regular vehicular entourage for the President and his staff. As we deplaned, an Air Force Officer, a Major singled me out and approached. He said, "Are you the TACSIGINT Officer?" He was asking me if I was the Tactical Signals Intelligence Officer, a near military equivalent to what I was doing. I replied, "Yes Major." He said, "Then you must be Ing. I'm Major Pappas with the Air Special Investigations Unit, I need to talk to you about what you saw up there, come with me Captain." I followed him into the terminal where we went into a room with a boat shaped oak table with four chairs around it. The room appeared to be a briefing room for pilots with its aeronautical charts on the walls, and electronic world time and weather display unit.

The Major opened a brown distressed leather dispatch case where he produced a printed copy of the report I had filed electronically while in the air, along with a brown leather clad investigators' notebook and sleek silver ballpoint pen. He handed me the printout of my report and said, "I want you to read this very, very carefully, is there anything else you want to add or may have noticed?" I took about a good five minutes reviewing the 10 printed pages in which I provided a chronological narrative of what had happened from my involvement and perspective. I wanted to be sure that nothing had been changed from the original report I had electronically filed. I was given the Major's permission to review the electronic version of the report still stored on my MARCO unit for reference. Everything seemed to be intact, unedited without external emendation. I handed the report back to the Major and said, "That's everything that I was aware of and able to report on."

He looked at me and said, "I don't have to remind you that your authorized security clearance level obliges you to maintain the Oath of Secrecy you signed under the Official Secrets Act, and this is one of those situations where full non-disclosure is in effect until the issue is deemed unclassified." What the Major really meant was that, until the matter was declassified for release under Freedom of Information, if ever, that the matter never existed publicly. I had been through these scenarios at least a dozen times in my professional career but I must admit, this one was a real mystery. Nonetheless, I acknowledged this, and we went through about 2 hours of a security debriefing on the incident which at the end left me with more questions than I was authorized to ask or to have answered and dare I say, even beyond the knowledge of the Major.

It was a few years later that I had stopped in to a local book store near Farragut Metrorail station in Washington, D.C. where I decided to waste some time before attending a meeting in the area. I had arrived for the meeting about 90 minutes early and decided to graze the covers of the magazines featuring women that only exist in the unidimensional world of fashion modeling and upscale style. I'm not talking adult men's magazines but actually the magazines that cater to mainstream entertainment, fashion and hair. I never look inside the magazines but just enjoy the covers. I always wonder why it is that I never see women like that in my neighborhood.

Anyway, after my magazine graze, I found myself standing by the new book section and just happened to pick up a book about conspiracy theories and there was an exact account of what had happened on the President's flight, summarized on the back cover as a teaser to buy the book. I purchased the book and found that the book, containing about eight chapters featured eight accounts of different incidents including the one I had personally witnessed, to others that had me wondering just how real some of the accounts were. In the chapter that covered the incident that I had been involved in, I was surprised to find several documents that had been released under Freedom of Information legislation with the requisite black marker gone wild over key text areas. You can imagine how surprised I was when one of the documents released was the printout of my original field report, reproduced in this book with black marker over my name and other details. I was famous but no one knew it!

The interesting thing that I had learned from reading the book was that the official line on this incident was that the unidentified object was a military test aircraft, with no further explanation. Apparently, according to the cockpit chronometer and a later inspection of the flight data recorder; navigation and communications systems were off line for 6 minutes, 9.44 seconds in our aircraft. That was about the length of time I would have estimated. The declassified ADVIS data report that was reproduced in the book identified the craft as being 269.4 feet in diameter with a height of 58.7 feet. This got me shaking my head; as by comparison, a Stealth F-117 military aircraft is approximately 65 feet in length, while a Boeing 777 Jumbo Jet is approximately 242 feet in length. That was a pretty huge craft for a military aircraft that could, in my opinion, easily out maneuver the 107 foot long, SR-71 Blackbird military aircraft, considered by military strategists to be the third fastest aircraft in the world at that time.

A few months later, I ran into a few other people that were involved in our project and being the devils' advocate, couldn't resist telling them about, and showing them the book I had found. At the end, we concluded that yes, it must have been a military test aircraft with ECM (Electronic Counter Measures) that could jam radio communications. However, we were puzzled at how fast and maneuverable this mystery aircraft was. Around that time, it was later hinted by the military press that a new version of Stealth Fighter was being developed, so we agreed, being the armchair experts that we were, that this was probably the bird. Of course, this was the easy path of least resistance approach that would keep everyone's feathers unruffled. The mystery still remains where this super maneuverable aircraft is today, or more importantly who has control of it and what they may do with it.

CHAPTER 4

▼

Operation Silent Eyes:
THE CAPITAL OBSERVER
AFFAIR

"Stupidity travels at the speed of light. Intelligent thought travels like a snowball gathering momentum and usually arrives too late but when it stops it becomes hauntingly inescapable."

—*Robert Ing*

It was about 2300 hours as I boarded the last Air Canada direct flight to the capital. It was February 13 and Metro City had nothing but freezing temperatures and snow squalls all day and evening. In the back of my mind I couldn't help but wonder if the flight would be cancelled and that I wouldn't be able to make it for the morning briefing in the capital. Whenever I fly, I like a window seat over the wing. I must be crazy, but there's no better view, night or day of a silver wing disappearing into the clouds or the horizon. Every time I see it, I think of the Led Zepplin tune, "Stairway to Heaven." In the half-hour that followed my boarding, it seemed like the ground crew a.k.a.

"ramp rats" had de-iced the wings of the aircraft no less than three times. The snow seemed relentless, as it kept on coming down, but melted as it hit the wing of the aircraft.

As the aircraft was secured for take-off, the flight attendants began their usual safety procedures briefing to the passengers. On this night you could actually feel the aircraft lumbering itself across the taxiway to the runway. It was as if gooey rubber cement had found its way onto the wheels of the aircraft. I decided that I was going to get comfortable and try to take a nap for the 55 minutes we would be in the air. However, this proved not to be the case. Seated next to me was a blond woman in her early to mid thirties who felt it necessary to tell me her life story. From this behavior it was apparent that she was traveling alone and felt nervous about flying. With the few opportunities I did have to contribute to the conversation, I did learn that this was only one of a small handful of flights that she had taken, that she was indeed nervous about flying and her name was Patricia.

The transition of our aircraft from terra firma to aeris was rocky but we made it and leveled off above the grey clouds. I could see the lights of the city below playing hide and seek between random openings in the grey billows. It seemed that my cabin mate, Patricia was all talked out as she leafed through an in-flight magazine and I decided that it was time to close my eyes. Of course, just then the flight attendants decided to break out the refreshments and circulate the usual fare of complimentary non-alcoholic beverages, potato chips and pretzels. It wasn't more than 6 minutes after being served that our aircraft hit some turbulence and abruptly bounced, at which point Patricia nervously grabbed my arm and yelled for all to hear, "We are all going to die." Two flight attendants came running to console her, as did I, having nothing short of a "Ninja death grip" on my arm. Of course, we were not going to die, and had just hit an air pocket. Everything was fine. Patricia, still nervous and very apologetic and embarrassed kept her head in a magazine for the duration of the flight.

The aircraft touched down in the capital without further incident. As I walked through the near vacant terminal, my footsteps and those of fellow passengers seemed to create a slight echo throughout the building as we were, it seemed, the last flight in. With just my carry-on bag, I beat many passengers to the rag tag airport limousines cued up to get the last spoils of the night. It was a fifteen minute ride from the airport to my hotel and the drive went by as quickly as my stroll through the terminal. The hotel I was booked in was a five star hotel and after registering I turned in, so I would be ready for the morning briefing at 0800.

The night didn't have enough hours for a restful sleep, but here I was sitting at a boardroom table relying on the mildest cup of coffee and blandest muffin I had ever experienced to keep me awake. It was 0800 hours and I was there with three other members of a project team that I had never met before. We were all waiting to be briefed on a new project that we knew nothing about. In some brief exchanges which included introductions, the only thing that was clear was that we were to work on some form of technology project involving data security. Around the table it became evident that we were all outside contracted talent specializing in different areas. Our team consisted of a digital forensics recovery specialist from Los Angeles, a physical security specialist from Ottawa, a criminal investigator from New York, and myself contracted as a forensic intelligence specialist.

It was now 0833, thirty-three minutes past the time our briefing was to begin and we were all getting pretty restless, and suffering from jet lag, just marking time. At that moment the door to the situation room opened and a middle aged gentleman followed by, to my surprise, Patricia, my flight companion from just less than a few hours ago. Patricia gave me a nod as she sat at the head of table. She introduced herself as a Project Officer and her sidekick as Project Coordinator. She then began by saying, "We have received all of your paperwork agreeing to participate in this operation. Your security clearances have been validated and at this time I must remind you that from hereon in, everything that will be communicated to you and your subsequent assignments are governed by the Official Oath of Secrecy applicable to your security clearances and the NDA (Non-Disclosure Agreement) that you have submitted."

She sounded almost like one of those lawyers that read the disclaimer on a radio contest advertisement but I kept this thought to myself. It was obvious she was new to this position and her partner's body language seemed to give the same impression about him as he played with his government issue black roller ball pen, gazing at the light fixture above the table. Her briefing, complete with black ink illustrations on overhead projected slides covered every piece of minutia from how we would report only to her or her sidekick, to how forms were to be filed. After about an hour of this "administration" boot camp she finally got down to the details of the project.

Apparently sections of data files containing sensitive pass codes and archived records seemed to be finding their way for sale and sometimes offered as free downloads on underground computer cracker (criminal hacker) websites and Internet user groups. Information such as passcode and algorithms to authenticate data content on identification cards as well as other operational data appeared to be of primary concern. The powers that be, worried that it may be one of their own, or even worse, a member of their CCF (Central Computing Facility) security staff who might be the culprit and were paranoid that an internal investigation might lead to a tip off resulting in the perpetrator disappearing. Further, as is almost always with the cases I have been involved in, calling in an outside agency to make an "official" inquiry (investigation) could lead to a media field day, erosion of public confidence and political ramifications. We were called in as private contract consultants to keep this one "under the radar screen" and everyone who sat around the table that morning knew that everything depended on this.

Our assignments were that each member of our team would take up the cover role of a business or information technology consultant around the CCF in order to study the processes of the staff that had direct or indirect access to the compromised data pool. Paying special attention to any anomalies that might appear. The one thing about information stored either magnetically or optically on a computer is that you can still look at the physical article, see that it is there but you never really know how many times it may have been copied and who has all those copies.

The CCF was truly a physical security fortress, located in a nondescript office building built around the 1930's on the outskirts of the downtown capital district. The building was restored and well maintained with its period brickwork, marble, brass, ornate Celtic knot accents and winged gargoyles on its upper exterior. From the outside it looked just like an old low rise 9 storey office building. However, once you passed through the heavy brass framed glass doors you found yourself in a lobby with the original marble floor and wall reaching up to an 18 foot ceiling complete with two fine Austrian crystal and brass chandeliers. Then, like a winter chill, at the end of the 50 foot long lobby stood a brushed silver finished steel wall with a 2 inch thick, 6 foot by 6foot bulletproof glass window and below it a small 2 foot by 2 foot steel door in which to pass small items to the armed officer on duty. To the left of this wall, a steel door operated by magnetic lock that lead into a small mantrap (a room of 5 foot square) where visitors would enter and then only when the outside door closed, an inside door at the other end could be opened allowing access to the facility. To the left of this door, two revolving doors constructed of steel frames and bulletproof glass where employees would swipe their access card and then place their thumb on a biometric reader in order to deactivate the lock on the door and gain entry. All the while, two armed officers maintained a vigilance with the aid of surveillance cameras and microphones mounted throughout the facility.

Once past the security barriers in the lobby, one would need either an access card or an escort with an access card to summon the elevator and to enter any other area. In the actual computer areas, it was apparent that the rooms themselves provided EMSEC protection. EMSEC is an acronym for Emissions Security, or what the non-government community refers to as TEMPEST (Telecommunications Electronics Material Protected from Emanating Spurious Transmissions). In the mid 1980's (yes, 1984 perhaps), Dr. Wim Van Eck (his real name), proved that electronic eavesdropping could be accomplished by using special receiving equipment that could intercept EM

(Electro Magnetic) fields generated in such things as computer monitors, television sets and many other electronic circuits. What this meant and still does today is if you are using your computer or watching television, I can be as far away down the block as several hundred meters and see everything on my "Van Eck" surveillance receiver screen that you are seeing on your computer or television screen without you knowing. As well, if you send a document to your printer, are playing or burning a CD or doing anything with information on an electronic device, chances are I can capture this data, view it, store it and analyze it at my leisure. This is known as Van Eck phreaking. The U.K. and U.S. Governments went to great lengths to perfect EMSEC in both areas of the ability to phreak (tap into) the devices of others and to protect devices of their own. Although over 20 years has passed since the identification of this technology, cost is a major reason why most electronic hardware is still not EMSEC secure. Anyone who has access to, or can afford an F1 classification ("Van Eck") receiver has the capability to intercept information this way. F1 classification receivers are restricted and controlled items maintained in the federal government intelligence agencies of both friendly and not-so-friendly nations. However, from time to time, construction plans and receivers do surface for sale in the underground, but these are typically for crude, basic instruments aimed at electronics experimenter hobbyists or the occasional espionage enthusiast. In the CCF, the risk of Van Eck phreaking was reduced by using RF (radio frequency) shield paint, tiles and wallpaper that would stop any EM (Electro Magnetic) waves from leaving or entering the secure area. RF shield paint and tiles are also used in high risk medical facilities where they do not want visitors using their mobile telephones while visiting patients as their use may interfere with life support or diagnostic equipment.

In my early days working in the field of SIGINT (Signals Intelligence) we used to line walls and ceilings with empty aluminum soda and beer cans (of a solid concrete floored room) to accomplish the same objective. Power lines and all other communications lines in the CCF computer rooms were also triple EM shielded by using three stage isolation transformers. There was no way that any form of EM signal spying was happening in these areas.

This facility was impressive from a physical security point of view. Computer systems that had to be connected to the outside world used secured and dedicated lines which passed through multiple stages of security buffer zones, known as DMZs and at least as many firewalls and security software checkpoints. However despite this level of security, computer logs indicated that on average, computer crackers attempted to gain unauthorized access to the system at the rate of 18 attempts every hour with about 60% of the attempts actually getting past the first DMZ. That's an average of 157,680 attempts per year with 94,608 successful security breaches! This may sound unbelievable or incredible to the general public, however, government and military computer systems are the obvious targets of crackers and are under constant siege by recreational crackers and information thieves. This issue is not taken lightly but while it is impossible to deter someone from the outside making an attempt of cracking the computer system, INFOSEC (Information Security) specialists do make the task of getting in much more difficult and those that do seldom get past the second or third (DMZ) security layer of a multiple (DMZ) security layer system.

Our team had assumed our cover roles as consultants within the facility and two weeks had gone by without incident. Then on a Wednesday morning we all attended a project meeting where we were informed that access card data that had been updated during those two weeks found its way onto an underground computer cracker site and was openly available for download. Embarrassed but not phased by this revelation our team began the investigation into how this may have occurred. After approximately a week into our inquiries, we had found some items of interest. One of my all time favorite quotes is from The Hound of the Baskervilles where Sherlock Holmes says, "The world is full of obvious things which nobody by any chance ever observes." In our case, this was truly suited to the occasion. Having exhausted all the possible ways for a technological security breach, a closer examination of the processes employed at the CCF revealed the weak link to be in the data back-up procedures. As with important data on any computer system, a back-up of the information is critical because ultimately a system will fail on average 1% of the time. Although this figure seems relatively small, just imagine if your own personal or business computer lost all of its information, how would this affect you? If you are like most people today, total information loss on a computer whether from having a hard drive crash to having the physical computer lost or stolen can have a major impact. Information on computers must be backed-up daily or at least weekly, depending on how often the computer is used, and the back-up copy must be stored in a separate area from the computer.

The CCF utilized a back-up rotation system where various data servers (computers with information on them) were backed up in accordance to a specific schedule during a 48 hour period.

As I had mentioned, the CCF was very impressive when it came to physical and data security; no one could gain access without anyone knowing and we had expected nothing less. However, we had soon discovered that the back-up copies made to magnetic tape of the information from the CCF computer systems were not encrypted. If you make a back-up copy of the information on your computer, generally that information can be read by anyone else who has the same computer program as you have unless you encrypt it. Encrypting your back-up makes the information appear as meaningless code if someone tries to copy or view it who does not have the passkey and special computer program to translate it back to useable information. An un-encrypted back-up maintained in another part of the secure CCF complex may have not proved to be a major security faux pas, but simply a flaw in the security process that could be easily remedied. However, the back-up tapes were shipped out to a lesser secured warehouse/storage facility across town by a bicycle messenger service! This exposed the information to unnecessary security risk while in transit and at the warehouse facility.

We were able to confirm that while the information on the back-up tape had been posted as a download on the Internet, the actual back-up tape had made its way to the warehouse facility. Our forensics team immediately retrieved the tape and began a thorough examination for trace evidence that could identify how and whom may have intercepted the tape and copied the data. After an exhaustive examination of the tape, we came up with very little and it soon became apparent that everything on the inside of the tape carrier including the tape had been handled using gloves, as the only thing out of the ordinary were traces of zea mays starch and tricalcium phosphate; a powder used on disposable latex gloves.

I then directed that we conduct an exterior chromopathic examination of the carrier. To be honest, I didn't really expect to find much given that the carrier would legitimately be handled by several people and no doubt bounced around picking up trace elements of thousands of substances. A chromopathic analysis involved subjecting the carrier to examination under varying frequencies of filtered light in order to accentuate any anomalies that may indicate special handling or tampering. When we chromopathically examined the carrier we had detected an identifying mark in the form of the alchemical symbol for sulphur; a circle divided into four equal sections by a cross. This mark was made on the adhesive paper address label on the carrier, in what could be considered in lay terms, invisible ink. The person who placed it there was sure to use a symbol that could only be put there intentionally as opposed to a more common single line type symbol that could be placed there by mischievous individuals. Invisible under common lighting conditions, the mark became visible when subjected to an ultra-violet light (UV) source at 390 nm (nanometers). Our next challenge was to identify the substance (ink) used to make the mark in the hope that it might lead us to the person who placed it there.

Further examination indicated that the invisible ink used contained dextran 70, polyethylene glycol 400, providone and tetrahydrozoline hydrochloride; put these all together and you have eyedrops. During the cold war, field intelligence operatives would carry a small bottle of eyedrops and cotton swabs, available at any pharmacist, drug or department store for the purpose of writing invisible messages. A single cotton swab would be used as a throw away pen with just one or two drops of this solution for writing a message. When dry this would produce an invisible message with an invisible longevity of three years or more, only visible under ultra-violet light of a specific wavelength. Invisible messages were often placed in the margins of ordinary letters home or the margins of a specific page in a bound book, on the inside of envelopes or back of a photograph to name a few ways that agents would get information back to their case or project officers. The advantage of using this simple arrangement for generating invisible messages is that a bottle of eyedrops and package of cotton swabs are readily available in most parts of the world and are not out of the ordinary items that would generate suspicion.

In expanding our inquiries, we retrieved the outgoing package log indicating the date and time the back-up tape had been picked up. Using the time from the log, we obtained an archival copy of the digital surveillance camera recording for the same time period. Reviewing the video of the security desk we were able to see the bicycle messenger as he walked up to the counter, signed for the back-up tape, all the while with his back to the camera. Then as he turned it appeared that the metal buckle of his messenger pouch caught the light of the overhead halogen ceiling light and reflected it back to the camera, temporarily creating what is known as "blooming" (overloading a camera sensor by a single intense light source) with the result being that the camera was temporarily blinded and was unable to record his face as he turned around and exited. Disappointed but undaunted by this minor setback, we retrieved the outgoing package logs for the past 12 months and cross referenced them to our messenger. We noted two other times when this messenger had made pick ups at the facility, both involving back-up tapes and on both incidents portions of the contents of the tapes were sold or posted on underground cracker websites. We retrieved the tape carriers and found the same invisible ink marking, made with eyedrops. We also retrieved the surveillance video for these two occasions and soon made the discovery that like the first video we viewed, the camera was temporarily blinded by blooming just as the messenger turned around to face the camera. As this seemed highly improbable that the available lighting in the desk area would happen to catch the metal belt buckle of the messenger pouch at exactly the same angle every time, we decided to analyze the videos. We attempted to locate the bicycle messenger through the messenger service but soon found out that the messengers were paid cash at the end of the shift for their trips and all one had to do was to show up at the depot with their bicycle for 0730, pick up a pager and you were good for the day. No records, no application, as the messengers were considered independent agents responsible for their own taxes and record keeping. In short, there was no way we could get paper on this individual, at least from the messenger service.

In analyzing the video, our forensics team had been able to identify the light source that caused the blooming of the camera was not mere coincidence. The lab determined that the source was from an LED (light emitting diode) laser with about 5 mW (milliwatts) output power at a wavelength of 530 nm (nanometers). What this meant in lay terms was that the surveillance camera had been temporarily taken out by a high priced green LED laser pointer; like the kind you might pick up in specialty audio-visual stores for close to $100.00. Although all video surveillance cameras utilize "anti-blooming" circuitry, even the best camera is no match if it is bombarded with a very strong focused beam of green laser light. Green, particularly around the 530 nm wavelength challenges even the best filtering circuitry as most of the normal signal coming from the camera's sensor is from the green element, therefore neutralizing the camera's imaging system. The concept of neutralizing color camera surveillance systems using green laser light is far from groundbreaking. Defense research institutes in the U.K. and U.S., have done extensive work on developing such systems using much more powerful green lasers in order to neutralize airborne and satellite based video surveillance systems. The findings of these top secret research projects are just beginning to become declassified and made available to the general scientific community and public.

From our analysis of the evidence; the invisible writing, and the use of a green laser to "zap" our surveillance camera, it was obvious that we were dealing with a group of individuals well versed in, or with access to anti-surveillance technology. Who they were and what motivated them was still unknown. To the untrained, the obvious solution of reverse tracking their trail from the underground computer (Internet) cracker boards seemed like an obvious choice, and our team did make subtle inquiries along this channel, but our mission was to find the ultimate leak within the CCF and real security threat. Much too often, in the heat of an incident or for political optics the knee jerk reaction of investigating and shutting down the distributors or users of criminal materials is executed with everyone being reassured that this criminal activity is no longer in our neighborhood, while the politico takes a bow and pat on the back. However, the manufacturer or source of the materials gets away and moves to, or may be in another jurisdiction to continue on with a new distribution network. Unfortunately, this is especially the case in international child pornography, drug and credit card fraud rings; we filter out or ban the outlets, and apprehend the users or distributors. What of the pornographer who actually solicits or takes the photographs of the subject? What of the supplier of the raw materials required to manufacture illicit drugs? What of the individual who actually hacks the credit card accounts? The source must be apprehended regardless of jurisdictional issues and the length of time it may take to execute an effective apprehension must be looked upon as an investment in a safer society. The only way to truly stop the crime under investigation is to apprehend the source.

Armed with our basic findings, we increased our internal surveillance, convinced that someone inside the facility was placing the invisible writing on the back-up tape carriers. We instituted a program where all back-up tapes were to be placed in a holding room, to await pick-up. Unbeknownst to staff, it was in this room where we subjected all tape carriers to a light source that would reveal the invisible ink marking if it were present, so we could track the tape ourselves.

It did not take long, once we knew what we were looking for, for one of our team members to notice an employee who had a bottle of eyedrops and a small box of cotton swabs in their desk drawer. This was noticed when the employee opened their drawer to retrieve a stapler during the normal course of their duties and the items in question were in plain view. The employee, Adolf Beck was a contract employee assigned to do general clerical duties at the facility.

A contract employee is an individual who does not work directly for the company they provide service for, but rather is hired by and works for another company, sometimes referred to as an agency or the contract employee may even be self-employed. These individuals are contracted through their agency or own company to come in and do work for the client company, in this case the CCF. The CCF enters into a service contract for a definite period of time; the agency invoices the CCF and in turn the agency pays the contract employee. With the privatization of many government services and downsizing of many corporations; contract employees are the alternative. A good example is in the area of forensics. Take for instance a small police department has a requirement about an average of once a month for a specialist in skeletal identification. If they were to hire this person, either on a full or part time basis they would have to pay the individual just to sit around and be available during the times there is no work for him or her, as well as pay employee benefits. However, as a contract employee, they could have the individual come in only when they are required and therefore only pay for the contract employee's time they actually use. Although the hourly rate for a contract employee may be as much as 30% to 50% greater than the rate they would pay a traditional employee, it is still cost effective as the client company only pays for the hours actually worked.

One of the major drawbacks in using contract employees in a security environment is that of screening and security clearances. While the majority of contract agencies do potential applicant pre-screening, the extent to which this is carried out varies. We contacted the agency that provided Adolf Beck requesting further information on him, under the pretense of doing a random security audit on our staff and facility. We were advised that under privacy legislation, Mr. Beck's employment application and resume could not be released or verbally disclosed without his written permission. As well, we did not have sufficient evidence to legally compel the release of this information. We decided not to push this issue as it might draw undue attention to our official inquiry.

Our next move was to examine the computer work station that Mr. Beck was assigned, in order to identify any indicators of questionable activity. Interestingly, 68% of North American corporations monitor and review the e-mails, voice-mails and company computer generated documents of their employees. The ability to do this legally in most jurisdictions is based on the premise that the employee is using someone else's property (computer, telephone system, company e-mail system) for the purpose of performing the duties of their job, not for personal or private pursuits. Therefore they cannot reasonably expect personal privacy or lay claim to intellectual property created, communiqués generated, transmitted or received on equipment or systems they do not own or subscribe to, particularly during periods when they are being paid for their time to conduct the business of their employer.

That evening I arrived at the CCF and proceeded to Mr. Beck's computer workstation. I booted the computer up using an external boot disk and then proceeded to make two bitstream copies of the hard drive assigned to him for analysis by our forensics team. When a computer user deletes a file it is not removed from the hard drive but becomes what is known as slack space or unassigned space on the hard drive. The computer will eventually overwrite (permanently delete) what is in the slack space, when a new file is saved in the same space but the larger the memory capacity of the hard drive, the longer the old "deleted" file may live until its space is required for a new saved file. The regular process of copying files from a computer, copies only the exact files specified, which is all that is really required for the majority of computer users. A bitstream copy will, however, copy the specified files plus the slack space between them. This means that even deleted files will get copied. Our bitstream copies would allow us to reconstruct and review any deleted files on this workstation back in our lab.

After several hours of analysis in the lab, we recovered Mr. Beck's deleted resume from his assigned hard drive. With information such as education and employment, we had sufficient information to conduct a background check. A computerized background check provided the expected result; the information on his resume could be substantiated and despite a minor discrepancy in residence addresses; thought to be more than likely a previous address, everything appeared as it should be. A criminal background check using the NCIC-CPIC computer database indicated that our suspect had no current or past criminal activity on file. We were also able to find excellent fingerprint impressions from Mr. Beck's workstation but were unable to find any matches in the available computer databases.

Undaunted by this dead end, I decided that some old school investigative work was required, if not just to satisfy me that I had done everything that I could in following up on the leads that were presented. I found out that the local Central Public Library maintained a collection of high school and university yearbooks. I went to the library with the hope that I could find Adolf Beck in his school or university yearbook and perhaps uncover more information about the man. As I perused the yearbook of his alma mater, I had hit paydirt. There he was in a grainy but all in all a fairly good black and white headshot photograph. There wasn't much more apart from the photograph, so I decided to go back to my office with a photocopy of his photo with the listing of his extracurricular activities below it in the hope that it would at least attest to the fact that I really did do some work on the case at the library.

When I arrived back at the CCF, my team had found a back-up tape with the tell-tale invisible eyedrop markings on its carrier waiting to be picked up. Anticipating this day would eventually come, we had placed two hidden pinhole cameras in the security reception area in order to capture the image of the courier. We also deployed our own plainclothes agents at strategic points in and outside the building in order to follow the courier to his destination.

Looking at the photograph from the university yearbook, I decided to scan it into the computer and use Electronic Facial Identification Technique (EFIT) software to age the photograph to see how accurate the software was, given that we already knew what Mr. Beck our suspect looked like. It was more of an idle curiosity on my part and admittedly, my own interest in playing with technology.

The result of the "morphing" of Mr. Beck's university photograph to his current age was very disappointing, as he did not at all look like the man we knew as Adolf Beck. At first, I thought to myself that this was a case of "failed by technology." However, given the specifications of this investigative tool and its accuracy rate, I began to doubt some of the very things we had accepted as verified fact about our Mr. Beck. I poured over our computerized checks of this individual and what really became more common was the fact the records that should reflect his current address, reflected an old, previous out of town address. I decided to run the previous address through the computer and cross reference it to its current occupants.

Upon doing this, to my surprise, the computer verification system indicated that Adolf Beck still lived there, and had done so for the previous 8 years. I then followed an impulse I had and called our Mr. Beck's previous employer from his resume, who also happened to be in the same city as the previous address of our Mr. Beck. I called the company and simply asked for Adolf Beck. The receptionist transferred my call, and I found myself listening to a voicemail message, "Hi, This Adolf, I am away from my desk but leave me a message and I will return your call."

Based on this new twist, it was obvious that our Mr. Beck, simply was not the real Mr. Beck, but who was he? I went back to the NCIC-CPIC computer database archives to determine if Adolf Beck had reported the theft or loss of a driver's license, passport or any other government issued document; as well as check for any report of identity theft. My search came up with nothing reported. I then proceeded to conduct a consumer credit bureau check of all three credit bureaus to see if there were any flags on Adolf Beck's credit record relating to stolen or lost credit cards, or perhaps an identity theft alert. This also came up a blank. What was interesting however, was that all three credit bureaus had the real Mr. Beck's address and his credit rating indicated that all his bills were paid on time without any problems past or present. This fact alone indicated that our Mr. Beck needed his assumed identity not for consumer credit fraud but in order to gain access to something he may not be able to do ordinarily, or perhaps he wanted to shield himself in some way.

It is a common practice of spies and terrorists to take on another's identity in order to gain access to information or places that they normally would be considered persona non grata. The perpetrator of such a maneuver is careful not to apply for credit cards as a credit check or credit report to a credit bureau may result. Rather they will opt for a debit card that makes use of the VISA or MasterCard network; also known as a prepaid debit card or secured credit card which will allow them to access services that require a credit card without a credit check. This will enable them to obtain such services as renting a video, getting a prepaid cellular telephone, car rentals or hotel reservations, etc.

When considering taking on another's identity the perpetrator will choose their mark (victim) carefully, ensuring that they lead a financially stable but uneventful, average lifestyle. Once a suitable individual is found, the perpetrator will learn all they can about this individual from likes and dislikes, childhood friends, recreational activities and lifestyle patterns. The perpetrator may befriend his mark, become a co-worker or become a client/customer of his target. This phase usually lasts no less than a year and can last several years, as dependent upon the extent this identity thief wishes to become his mark. A detailed study is a must in order to avoid detection later in the game. Towards the end of this relationship with the mark, the perpetrator will begin to obtain either legitimate copies of, or forged copies of identification documents bearing his marks' name such as birth certificate, driver's license, library card, prepaid debit card, etc. Once these items are secured, the perpetrator will then either modify a real copy of his marks' resume or create one from the facts he already knows. Armed with the knowledge and documents, the perpetrator then becomes his mark, in another city, state, province or country. He will gain employment, obtain a residence and live his life as any ordinary citizen using his new identity.

At this time it was obvious that our Mr. Beck did this in order to gain access to information, but the three burning questions were; what was the real identity of this imposter, what information was he after and for what purpose?

The back-up tape remained waiting for pick-up for two days until a bicycle messenger came around to collect it. It came as no surprise that the messenger "zapped" the security camera as he always did, but this time we were able to obtain two very good digital images of his face from our hidden pinhole cameras. As he exited the building, our surveillance teams followed him, and we were able to send the digital images of our courier to their mobile telephones so they could confirm who they were following. The path the messenger took had him winding his way along busy downtown streets. Our team was undaunted and never lost sight of him. The messenger double-backed circling around several city blocks. Our team thought that they had been made (identified as following the target) but it soon became apparent that this was just a ritual, a habitual precaution that gave the messenger a false sense of security and nothing more. The final destination was a bicycle shop, whose entrance was in a back laneway. Oddly enough that laneway backed out onto to a street that had a Department of Defense Armory just across the street. Our team observed the messenger carry the back-up tape in and then about an hour later leave with the tape and then deliver it to the designated archive warehouse where it was intended to be delivered. The surveillance team then followed the messenger on several other pick-ups without incident, at this point to go any further would have tipped off our target so the team broke off the surveillance.

Meanwhile back at the CCF, we had arranged that the messenger use a special pen to sign the delivery chit and from this pen we were able to obtain two very good fingerprint impressions of our messenger. Armed with the fingerprints we ran them through the NCIC-CPIC database but came up with nothing. The digital images we had taken of the messenger were analyzed and compared through the Eigenimage System and from there we were able to identify the messenger through digital driver's license images (photographs) through the Bureau of Motor Vehicles. We identified the messenger as Peter Lesurques and were able to obtain a current address and set up our surveillance team at his residence. I was feeling lucky and decided to run our Mr. Beck's CCF employee identification photograph through the Eigenimage System. Sure enough we had a match to the expired Bureau of Motor Vehicles driver's license database. His real name was Joe Vaux. Upon further investigation of the real backgrounds of these two individuals we had discovered that they were members of an underground Internet computer Cracker group whose sole purpose was to infiltrate high security systems for the purpose of bragging rights and as a secondary motivation—profit from whomever would purchase the spoils of their endeavors. We checked, double checked and validated these individuals to confirm that there were no terrorist ties, motivations or sympathies in their past or current known activities. These individuals were strictly motivated by "fame" within their peer group and cash.

The Eigenimage Facial Recognition System uses any digital photograph or traditional paper printed photograph which is then converted to a digital photograph by scanning it into a computer. Images of individuals may be obtained from existing criminal, driver license, passport, or employee photographic identification databases or even from newspapers, magazines, corporate brochures and websites. Unobtrusive images of individuals may also be obtained from video surveillance systems in airports, bus terminals, shopping malls, parking garages, commercial and residential buildings thus eliminating the need for cooperation on the part of a suspect. Eigenimage takes an image and converts it into numerical data and compresses it so that the image is accurately identified as a unique linear numerical sequence or in lay terms a digital serial number. By comparing the digital serial number of a suspect's image to that of others stored in an Eigenimage System database, a computer match may be found. Once found, the image is compared both by computer and manually by a real person to validate that there is a positive match.

Based on the evidence against Joe Vaux, his known affiliations and the fact that he had passed himself off as Adolf Beck with fraudulently obtained and false identification, our team had what we needed to apprehend and detain this subject. Upon taking Joe Vaux into custody we executed a search on the bicycle shop and retrieved large quantities of computer equipment, including duplicating equipment capable of copying the back-up tapes used by the CCF. During the execution of the search we were also able to apprehend other individuals in the process of illegally accessing other restricted government and corporate networks and databases. Peter Lesurques was also apprehended and detained for his part in intercepting and duplicating the back-up media. A search was also executed on Peter Lesurques' residence where even more sophisticated computer equipment was seized.

In tracing the serial numbers of the computer accessory equipment, we soon discovered that none of these items were actually purchased or reported stolen. In interviews with those we apprehended, an interesting scheme of obtaining computer accessory equipment was revealed. Members of the Cracker group would routinely go into any major department store with a computer equipment section and locate the product they required on the shelf. In the interest of inventory control and logistics many computer accessory manufacturers place a label on the outside of the box with information containing the item's serial number, version number and electronic identifier.

The perpetrator makes a note of all of this information, plus of course the obvious such as make, model and catalogue number of the desired device. He or she then goes home and seeks out the website of the product manufacturer. As most medium to high-end computer equipment comes with a 30 day to 1 year warranty, manufacturers give purchasers an option to validate their warranty by either mailing in a card that is inside the product box or going online and doing this via their website. Our perpetrator, although not having purchased the item goes online, armed with the serial number and other detailed product information that most assume (often including the manufacturer's customer service department) would only be known to someone who had purchased the product, broken the seal on the box and installed it.

The perpetrator then proceeds to register the product under an assumed individual or company name with a temporary mailing address such as a mailbox or package receiving service. Approximately a month later or more the perpetrator will call the manufacturer's warranty service department complaining that the accessory device does not work, at which point he or she will be instructed to send the unit back for free warranty service. Our perpetrator gets a box puts padding in it, tapes it up, opens and closes it up, re-tapes it and does this several times. After the box appears that it may have been subjected to unauthorized entry or damage, the empty box is addressed to the warranty department and sent out insured with a tracking number through a postal or courier service. Whether the perpetrator hears from the warranty department or not a telephone call is initiated and the tone of the call is a very unhappy, disappointed customer ready to go to the top to get resolution. What usually happens because on all outward appearances a product malfunctioned, then was lost and the customer has suffered, the warranty department will send the perpetrator a new unit and the perpetrator may even claim the insurance on the lost article. This is how many terrorists and underground criminals have obtained products to further their technological criminal activity. Of course at the time of this writing, all of this is and always has been highly illegal, and today is much more detectable by internal corporate security departments and law enforcement.

CHAPTER 5

▼

Operation Sidetrack:
THE PAPER TIGER AFFAIR

"There comes a time in life when you realize you know much more than those around you. However, you also realize that you may never have the opportunity to use this knowledge for the benefit of anyone. So you live each day as it comes, detached from the things that you know you could change."

—Robert Ing

The civil war had taken its toll on the locals. For centuries neighbor had fought neighbor and justified it as a holy war to rid their homeland of tribal and religious extremists. To a first world armchair observer reading the scattered news reports throughout the western media it looked like there were only occasional spurts of violence with hundreds of faceless casualties without a life, personality or families. The western media when it selects to report on a story of suffering from overseas always seems to sanitize it from the reality that these are real lives, real people with families no matter whose side they are on.

Regardless, here I was in the thick of it. In a city that had been bombarded by mortar shelling and continued to be. The bloody lifeless bodies lay strewn in the streets amongst the rubble. At first glance they just looked like dirty piles of soiled clothing until you got up close and could see bloody limbs, fragmented heads covered with blood, and shrapnel, blackened by fallout. The mortars did not discriminate from soldiers, civilians, radicals, women, children or infants. This was the civil war that never quite got reported in the west, at least to this extent.

I had only landed a week ago but it seemed like months. The smell of blood and death; of decaying human remains permeated the dry hot air like a low hovering fog that refused to lift. My mission objective was to observe and if a western national were to get into trouble, become injured or killed, to provide intelligence on the incident and in the latter situation assist in the positive identification of the individual through fingerprinting, and in more severe instances in the retrieval of remains for forensic identification. There were only about six of us charged with this task but with the provision of a handful of western civilian relief workers supervising the locals on the surface it appeared like a manageable task. Normally, western aid volunteers would probably be left to their own devices in these relief operations but as many of the volunteers here seemed to have family ties of sorts to many of the socially and politically well entrenched back home, most of our team knew why we were sent here.

The mission was briefed as a 90 day support deployment and seemed simple enough. However, being briefed about the conditions and then actually being there was a completely different matter. Officially, as far as the nationals, the military and host government was concerned, we were there just to observe and assist with providing casualty aid when things would get rough. We worked alongside the military field militia unit and were given access to their limited medical facilities. On quiet days, times when the shelling was heard but not felt, typically seven miles out, I and some of my team members would teach emergency first aid and CPR (Cardio-Pulmonary Resuscitation) procedures to the local able bodied civilian population in preparation for the next time when their families or neighbors may become the casualties of a faceless attack from the sky.

The definition of first aid is the help given to an injured or suddenly ill person using readily available, improvised materials. I remember back in Canada and the United States whenever I taught a first aid class how I would emphasize to my students that just because you didn't have a first aid kit didn't mean you couldn't perform first aid. Likewise, I would follow up with the line that just because you had passed a first aid course with a first aid wallet certificate in your pocket didn't mean you were obligated to do Chapters 1 to 27 on your casualty. To further emphasize this to my students, I was the only instructor, as far as I knew that taught to civilians what was known in the military as the "O Squared Rule." That is, "Only if your comfortable to do so, and Only if it's safe to do so." Or should I say, at least using that particular phrase.

In this part of the world survival truly meant the ability to improvise and be creative with what was available. Bandages were scarce and in an emergency the cleanest bandage available may end up being the sweaty shirt off of someone's back, and if you were lucky, perhaps off of a live someone. Water was a priceless commodity that was rationed, so if you had access to water during an emergency you had better be sure that the wound in question really needed cleaning. This was the state of affairs, where people died from infection complications associated with injuries we in the west would consider minor because we had the water, supplies and antibiotics to reduce infection risk. However, the people never stopped trying to survive, to live.

No matter whose side you are on in a conflict, the average person just wants food, shelter, and clothing for themselves and their families. The problem is that when you displace a person by removing the opportunity to obtain any of these basic essentials, or destroy their family they then become disenfranchised individuals with virtually nothing to lose—not even their own life and they become easy prey to the radical political, religious or criminal whims of others. On the ground, in this place, we had more than our fair share of such individuals. Whether it is in the deserts, the jungles or inner cities, there is no individual more dangerous to a community and civilized society than a person with nothing to lose. These are the pawns, the human sacrifices and thugs that give up their humanity and own lives to become self-destructive human killing machines on the orders of manipulative cowards that lead from a safe distance in the rear, only moving forward and out of the shadows to seize the spoils of chaos when it is safe for them to do so.

The national group to whom the west had allied itself with wanted to stabilize the region. However, this would be an expensive proposition in terms of collateral lives (the killing of innocent civilians and military allies who got in the way), the dollars needed to execute such an action, and the political implications on the world stage. The national group felt that she had to protect her own at any cost and that the lives of the enemy whether military or civilian were worthless. Of course they could not come out and publicly or officially allow this position to be known but it was obvious given their actions and rhetoric. As a member of an intelligence team on the ground, this position became clearer and clearer as the days went by on my deployment.

A local merchant, who went by the name of Malek had taken to me and offered to help "get anything I desired," was a character that even to this day I will remember. He was a person with connections who, despite shortages of supplies and being in a war zone, could within a week's time find whatever it was a person would want and of course, sell it for an inflated price. He had no political or military connections. He was truly an entrepreneur of survival just trying to feed his family and make the best of the worst situation imaginable. Due to his ability to get scarce items for people, he was able to obtain access and mobility in an area where most were restricted or forbidden to go. Everyone knew him.

Strict martial law enacted six years ago had caused all radios owned by civilians to be seized and destroyed. However, with the passage of time, this prohibition was lifted but radios for civilian use were so scarce that the ones that were available were sold for ridiculously high prices. For instance, a small transistor radio found in many discount stores in North America selling for US$5.00 was commanding a price of US$100.00! Of course, if you could afford or had a radio, the next big hurtle was affording the batteries as power from mains (electrical power) was simply not available. A relief coordinator, Nehasa at the local orphanage told me a story of how she wished she could hear the BBC but lost her radio during the prohibition but that it didn't matter anyway as she couldn't afford batteries. Nehasa was a native, who lived at the orphanage taking care of the children literally 24 hours a day. I decided that I would do something for her, as a gesture of goodwill. My first ever deal with Malek was to scrounge some materials I needed for what I wanted to give to Nehasa. When I met with Malek, I gave him a very short list of the items which he looked at and exclaimed, "This is just garbage. Don't you want some wine, cigarettes, bottled water, chocolate or a woman?" I replied, just get me the items on the list and he looked at me as if I was crazy. He replied, "OK, since this is your first time I only charge you twenty US dollars, but I won't be so easy next time. "We haggled for about 15 minutes and I ended up paying him ten US dollars. About a week later he gave me a box with the items I had requested. This transaction with Malek became the start of about half a dozen more during my deployment and a business association that would never be forgotten.

I gathered the parts Malek was able to get me and pieced them together with other odds and ends I was able to scavenge from battlefield debris. The result was a shortwave radio that did not require batteries and that was capable of receiving the BBC as well as other shortwave stations.* I made this specifically for Nehasa and presented it to her the next day after I made it, much to her surprise. Although crude by western standards this radio worked exceedingly well, largely due to the fact that there were no local commercial radio stations for miles to cause interference. One of my specialties back home was the area of Improvised Technology. Improvised Technology involves the art and science of calling into service common objects or to redesign/retrofit existing technology to create or build a different device. Like taking a handful of odds and ends and building a shortwave radio that required no batteries. When not deployed in the field, I would provide instruction on Improvised Technology to federal and corporate protective service personnel in the west. To this day, I still provide instruction in this area despite the availability of an ever increasing range of high technology intelligence and surveillance devices.

As a result of my relationship with Malek, we shared a camaraderie that only survivors in a real living purgatory could appreciate. One day, Malek came to me with a concerned look on his face. I was already expecting some sort of sales pitch for some rare find that he was going to give me the benefit of first refusal on. However, instead he insisted that we go to some place private as he had something very important to tell me. I obliged him and we found ourselves at the back of a makeshift latrine. After much beating around the bush, I said, "Malek, you must come to the point. What is it that you need to tell me or ask me?" Malek said in a whispered voice, as his eyes seemed to scan everything in sight, "Mr. Robert, you are a good customer and valued associate. I tell you this for I fear for you. Please do not be present in the old city tomorrow afternoon." I asked him for more details but he would tell me nothing, and excused himself only saying, "please do as I ask", as he scurried away. This left me curious more than anything else but I decided to be mindful of what I had been told. I thought about what was in the old city. The old city was the far eastern district of the city. Thinking it through, nothing much was there, some old buildings, displaced settlements and a scattering of civilian relief camps. No military or government targets. I figured it must be some sort of protest by the displaced locals or something.

That evening the shelling seemed to be not as aggressive as it had been, and the reduced noise level seemed to make it more difficult for me to settle in for the night. The human body is a strange thing. Once you get used to an annoyance it seems more annoying when it's not present. Despite this I did manage to get some sleep. The next day was pretty much like the others. Escort the western relief workers around to various parts of the cities. My team members and I looked at it as riding shotgun at times, as many of the locals; the very people we were allegedly there to help seemed to want no part of us and at times would demonstrate this quite aggressively. Some would hurl rocks and other debris at us, while others would just stand and spit repeatedly while shaking their clenched fists. It was a little after 1300 hours and my partner said that a medical relief worker asked if we could shuttle her up to Relief Camp E-7, as she had some vaccines she wanted to administer there before sundown. So the three of us headed off to the relief camp and making good time, we arrived with only 40 minutes traveling time. The medical relief worker made her way into the camp, and at that point I heard the sound of a small engine above our heads. Looking up, it appeared to be an unmanned reconnaissance drone. My partner looked at me and said, "It's from across the border, an ally. No one else runs drones here. He's probably just doing some visual reconnaissance to see who's here." The drone made several low level passes. To be honest, I thought that it was actually going to hit the Red Cross and UN flags flying over the relief camp as it came in so close. About fifteen minutes passed and the sound of shelling began, getting louder and closer with each volley. All of sudden shells began to hit the relief camp, people began running for their lives in every possible direction. I spotted our relief worker, grabbed her and hurried her into our vehicle along with a mother and child to whom she was attending. My partner and I literally tore up the road on our escape away from the shell attack in the area of the relief camp. As we made our hurried exodus with debris flying all around us, my partner said look up there, "it's the damned drone." I looked back at the relief worker, only to find that she had a small digital camera, taking pictures of what was happening. Shrapnel in the form of small stones and sand grazed us as we diligently drove for our lives. Ironically, as we got about a kilometer away we seemed to be free of all shelling activity. At that point, I recalled what Malek had said, and yes we were definitely in the old city at the wrong time.

It became apparent that the shelling of the relief camp was intentional. When we arrived back at base, we reported the incident to the Commanding Officer and went through the usual debriefing. About a week later, the story of the shelling of an unidentified relief camp in our region made the news. The official line was that it originated across the boarder as part of that allied nations' assistance to neutralize a military target in the region. Apparently, the Minister of Defense and his General of the Army stated that it was an unfortunate targeting error and that they had no way of knowing that a relief camp with innocent civilians had fallen to the shelling. The shelling of the camp cost 67 civilian lives; mostly women and children.

Of course to those on the ground in the region, it was common knowledge that the eastern part of the old city had no military targets but simply relief camps and aid facilities. Further, there was the question of the drone. It became evident that the drone would have been able to identify, using its digital cameras that the target in question was a civilian target. As well, in shelling operations, a drone has only one real purpose, to ensure accuracy in the kill. The digital photographs taken by the relief worker provided very clear images of the drone, which my partner and I were able to confirm was operated by the allied border nation in question. Copies of the photographs were submitted with a follow-up report to our Commanding Officer, but no further reference was made to them. The medical relief worker filed a report a few days later that her camera had been stolen and about a week after that she had been RTU (Returned to Unit) back home, in this case England.

A brief mention was made in the media that a drone had been spotted prior to, and during the shelling by an anonymous source but the neighboring allied nation's Ministry of Defense denied that any drone had been deployed or was even available the day of the shelling. The spotting of the drone was downplayed as an observational error made by an untrained civilian in the heat of the excitement. Politicians on both sides had a media field day and resolutions were proposed to increase western aid in the way of arms and armaments to "the good guys" so that mistakes like this would not be made again. At least that is what it really boiled down to at the end of the day. Of course, the wheels of bureaucratic administrations do turn slowly and while much was agreed to "in principle", fortunately the increase of arms and armaments would see a delay of at least a year. This meant that there still might be a slim chance that many of the locals would at best live long enough to see their next birthday. Needless to say this outraged those stakeholders who believed that stabilizing the region was the only way to ensure peace.

It was day 27 of my 90 day deployment but who was counting. Already I had witnessed firsthand how paranoia, power, politics and technology can kill innocent bystanders.

This was no isolated case from what I had heard from the locals, but there was very little I could do about it. I had a part to play just like everyone else, with the hope that I might at the very least be able to balance out the odds throughout my lifetime in other places at another time. These things happen everyday, somewhere in the world, maybe even in your neighborhood to some degree; don't fool yourself. Just be thankful and pray that it may never permeate your small circle of reality.

I hadn't seen Malek making his usual appearances every couple of days. A rather unkempt man, with the appearance and aroma of a homeless beggar approached me. I actually had been trying to avoid him, as I did not want to contribute to his endeavors that day. Nonetheless, he stood in front of me and said, "Are you Mr. Robert?" Surprised that he knew my name and not knowing what to expect, I hesitantly said, "yes, I am."

"I am Mustafa, Malek told me to deliver message to you." The man said in broken English, as he pulled his right hand out of the front waistband of his trousers and motioned it as to shake hands with me. I said, "How is Malek, I haven't seen him for awhile," trying to focus on speaking to the man, while making the motion that I had some substance on my hand that would hinder me from shaking his. Mustafa told me that Malek had left the region as he was finally granted immigration to France. Before Malek left he had instructed Mustafa to deliver a very special message to me. "Malek says what happened in the old city will happen again but to your first place, maybe on Tuesday. Do you know what he is saying?" Mustafa said with an inquisitive but puzzled look on his face. I knew exactly what Malek was trying to tell me but I would not betray his confidence. I replied, "It must be another one of those parties."

I gave Mustafa a small, but expected token of appreciation for his trouble and sent him on his way.

When I first arrived in the region, I had been assigned to keep an eye on a small orphanage that housed widowed mothers and their children. It was outside this small home that I met Malek for the first time and I recall he had actually said to me, "so this is your first place here in the city." I recalled his exact words and still had vivid images of the shelling that he warned me about. I also thought that the small house would be absolutely no match for the shells and that there would definitely be no survivors. But who could I tell, who would believe me? The first attack was obviously sanctioned by someone high up, so as to get greater western intervention in the region. If the information that I received was true, this meant that someone, somewhere wanted to turn up the heat to get intervention faster at the cost of innocent women and children. Besides, there is nothing more moving than seeing the bloody corpses and cries of child survivors on the late night news. I resolved that this was something that I could not stand by and hear about on the evening news.

It was Tuesday morning about 0600, my partner and I were supposed to go make our rounds and be on field standby as per post orders. I decided today was the day I had to play my own agenda. We were normally assigned a Type 2 ambulance but I convinced the Transport Sergeant on duty that there seemed to be a clutch problem with our vehicle and asked if we could take the much larger Type 4 ambulance instead. After a long whine on my part he let me take the vehicle just to get me out of his hair. My partner looked at me as if I was completely crazy that morning. My partner, Nicos was a quiet sort of fellow and had only been in the service for about a year out of GMT (General

Military Training) but he was a very competent, reliable individual. I was about five years his senior in age and was more the "ego" of our team. Nicos was a short form for his real name which was so long, the embroidered web name tape on his combat uniform went from almost under the armpit right to the very edge of where it was buttoned in the front. His name was even harder to pronounce, so everyone just called him Nicos. I turned to Nicos and I said, "I have something I have to do today, that may be very dangerous, even fatal. I can't get into details but you can stay behind if you want to." Nicos looked at me and said, "We are partners, I know you wouldn't risk your ass just for the hell of it. So whatever this thing is you must do, let's get going." During the time I had spent with Nicos, he knew me and I knew him. You cannot be in a situation where so much death and destruction exists without having a bond and connection with the very person you depend on to cover your back and you theirs. I knew he was down for it, and I knew I could depend on him.

We pulled out of the compound. Nicos drove as I took the lookout position. I instructed Nicos to take us to the orphan house. He looked puzzled but headed that way. When we arrived, the residents were just getting their breakfast. You could hear the infants crying and children making the sounds children make when they are in their fantasy play land. I instructed the house mothers that we came to take them on an outing for the day. They looked at me like I was crazy. Must have been my day for people thinking I was crazy. Anyway, it appeared that some of the mothers did not want to leave on this impromptu trip and despite my urging some were firmly determined to stay at home that day. I felt time was running out, if something was going to happen. I could not convey what I knew because I had no confirmation of what might happen. Everything I was doing was in contravention to my orders, and if something did happen it was at the hands of some faceless higher ups who were supposed to be "the good guys."

So we packed up the mothers and children we had and drove off. I had a sinking feeling inside as I looked back in the rearview mirror to see the images of some of those we left behind that insisted on staying. This time I was doing the driving. As we drove along the road out of the city, we observed two large canvass covered trucks that looked suspicious. Nicos and I looked at each other and after a brief discussion decided that it was either an illegal arms shipment or refugees hiding under the canvas covers. It wasn't long until we heard distant gunfire. Unlike the sporadic shots here and there we were used to hearing, these were volleys and lots of them. As we continued making our way out of the city, we drove past yet another canvas covered truck with an extremely large antenna mounted on the back. The truck turned and began heading in our direction. I sensed trouble.

The truck roared up the dirt road creating a dust trail that could be seen for miles. I hit the accelerator; I knew we had been made. The closest outpost was a British command post about 12 kilometers out. The canvas truck came to life as hooded figures in battle fatigues threw off the canvas that they were lying underneath in the bed of the truck and started firing at us. In their native language, someone yelled several times, "kill the women and children." As I drove furiously, Nicos attempted to return fire with a submachine gun and sidearm we had onboard. Fortunately our vehicle was more maneuverable than our assailants and they only had semi-automatic rifles.

Nonetheless, they were gaining on us. This drive seemed to last a lifetime, but we came upon the command post and as we got into visual range our assailants broke off the chase and disappeared. Pumped up purely on adrenaline we sped into the command post. A Warrant Officer and three of his men came running to our ambulance. He said, "My god man you have been hit." Not knowing what he was referring to I looked down and the floor mats were covered in blood. I recall saying there's people in the back, and then I passed out.

The next thing I recall is waking up in an infirmary bed, with Nicos in the bed next to me. We were both alive. We would both pull through. I took three rounds, one in my right lower back, one in my right buttocks and one in my ankle. Nicos took two, one in his left thigh and one in his left shoulder. When the Warrant Officer came in, I asked him about our passengers. He looked at the floor with a grim face. He told me that the interior floor and walls of the vehicle had been covered with blood and that out of the 9 women and 13 children, only 4 women and 9 children survived. He then asked, "Were you from the orphan house in the city?" I answered, "Yes, we were", at which point I suspected that I was going to be placed in custody by the Military Police for the whole fiasco. The Warrant Officer then said, "You are bloody lucky. Everyone at that place was massacred by guerrillas. They say no survivors, but it appears you lot have just changed that to 13. Good job." I was numbed to think that those women, the infants and children had all been slaughtered.

Being confined in the infirmary for a few days, I received a visit from our Commanding Officer. He literally read me the riot act and threatened to have me charged and held accountable for what happened aboard our vehicle. He literally waived the judicial inquiry request papers in my face as he stormed out. However, I did not regret what Nicos and I did, for we were able to save the lives of at least 13 people. If given the opportunity again, I know that my partner and I would have done it again.

The following week, Nicos had a visitor. The man appeared out of place with his "too new" looking green work dress uniform. His pants had a press that could give a paper cut to anyone that would brush up against them. There was no rank or unit insignia on the jacket and his boots had absolutely no wear or tear on the heels or pebble textured black leather uppers. It was apparent by his looks that he had gone to great extremes to fit in but really didn't. He had chatted with Nicos for what seemed to be over an hour at which point he had left. I approached Nicos and asked him about his visitor. He told me that the man was from the State Department and had asked him questions about our little field trip. Nicos told me that he was instructed neither to mention his conversation with anyone nor to tell anyone about what happened. Nicos was given his transfer papers and would be on a flight bound for home on Friday.

On Thursday, I received my orders by messenger direct from agency headquarters. My instructions were also to return home and stapled to the official document was a letter congratulating me on the successful completion of my mission and terminating my engagement in the operation. From all this I assumed that there would be no judicial inquiry because we did the right thing, for the right reasons.

The next day, Friday, Nicos and I were at the airfield and said our goodbyes as we prepared to board separate aircraft bound for opposite directions. We joked and recollected our recent experiences. We shook hands and went our separate ways. After a flight of several hours, the grey military air transports lined up on the apron along the taxiway at the airport looked like a welcome sight as my aircraft cruised across the tarmac toward the terminal. I thought how truly great it was to be home and how lucky I was to be a natural born citizen of this great country. Having deplaned, I eased my very sore body through the terminal over to the commercial airlines waiting area to connect to the commercial airliner that would see me touch down in my hometown in about an hour. After checking in and getting my seat assignment, I sat in the waiting area and happened to glance at a copy of the days' newspaper. I picked up the paper and began grazing over the contents. There on page A-19 was a small article that reported due to heightened violence against civilians in the city (I had just left), that Western military aid would be fast tracked and further increased. The small article made mention of how guerillas had stormed an orphanage and slaughtered all inhabitants. The aid package, the article continued, would include a heightened military presence, weapons and financial assistance. I thought to myself how real life and death perceptions and situations at times seemed to be a mere macrocosm of a microcosmic chess game.

One thing was for sure, Nicos and I both knew that whatever had happened on the ground the day we were under fire, that we could take comfort in that we did all we could to make a difference. Neither of us had regrets, or were fearful for our actions that day. In this world, no matter where you are or what your role may be, you will be given an opportunity to do something that will change the life of at least one person. The hardest part of your mission is not finding such an opportunity but recognizing it.

*For construction plans to build Nehasa's Radio please see Appendix A

The author in 1974.

INTERNATIONAL POLICE CONGRESS

WASHINGTON, DISTRICT OF COLUMBIA

To all who shall see these presents, Greetings:

KNOW YE, That reposing special trust and confidence in the integrity and ability of

Robert S. Ing

We do hereby appoint the above as a

SPECIAL AGENT

Of The

INTERNATIONAL POLICE

CONGRESS

and do empower same to fulfill the requirement of such appointment according to the Operative Rulings of the System, to have and to hold said Appointment with all the privileges and emoluments there unto of right appertaining for the term as set forth in the Registration Card issued Annually hereunder from date hereof.

In testimony whereof, we have caused these letters to be made Patent and the Seal of the International Police Congress to be hereunto affixed.

Done at the City of Washington, D.C., in the year of our Lord,

MAY 23 1983

INTERNATIONAL POLICE CONGRESS

By *Melvin W. Berds*

EXECUTIVE DIRECTOR
P.O. Box 570552
Miami, Florida 33157

The author's certificate of appointment as a Special Agent in 1983.

The author with one of his favorite vehicles in 1992.

A video still from a forensic evidence recovery instructional workshop conducted by the author in 2001.

CHAPTER 6

▼

Operation Consparanoia:
THE INVISIBLE GROUP
AFFAIR

"The truth alone has never set anyone free. It is only doubt which will bring mental emancipation."

—Anton Szandor LaVey

On every corner of the street Militiamen stood in their combat fatigues holding submachine guns like a mother would cradle her newborn. Their presence was commanded in preparation, and for the duration of the world leader's summit to be held in the city. For the next three days the city would be host to men so powerful and representing so much wealth that they could easily buy the entire host country. The location was selected by committee two years ago, based on the political climate, general security and no doubt weather of the region.

The world leaders at this summit consisted of the national leaders of democratic, socialist and communist countries as well as members of the world's monarchies. It is interesting to consider that in most democratic nations, the general consensus is that the people elected by their citizens are done so at the will of the electorate majority. However, long before the "democratic" process takes place; those that ultimately will be the choices to be the leadership and national face of a democratic country are selected and groomed by insiders far removed from the concerns of the average citizen electorate. The candidate options put forth for consideration by the mass citizenry have already been prescreened to ensure that regardless of their political party stripes that they all have read the right book, went to the right school, and regrettably are in bed with the same crowd as their "good friends" (a term used in the ivory towers to describe a public opponent or adversary but a pub mate in private). Perhaps the day may come when someone who has actually read the wrong book and went to all the wrong schools becomes a President, Premier or Prime Minister. In any case, the poor person that does get elected to lead a country is really just a figurehead with an exceptional salary and benefits package. The real power and policy lies with the unelected advisors who are high ranking salaried civil servants, not allied with any political party. These are the people, the Geppettos who utilize elected Pinocchios to be the faces and messengers of political will, with all its slings and arrows.

World leader summits although a publicized meeting of national leaders, are also a meeting of unelected policy advisors. While the will of the electorate should establish the tone of foreign policies in a democratic state, the preambles to many agreements regarding foreign policy, the world economy and environment are already established by the time one of these summits ends. The summits themselves may take the form of formal meetings and conferences at a lavish venue or may be at a luxurious resort getaway, where the "boys" informally discuss who to sanction and what direction interest rates should go over a glass of Osborne vintage port and an Arawak President cigar. This is not to say that such summits are unnecessary or wasteful, although excessive they are needed to coordinate the collective government of the world. Did I say world government or government of the world?

My role was a very minor one in the grand scheme of things and that was just to deploy and oversee a token handful of uniformed security guards that would more or less act as a psychological physical security deterrent and frontline security concierge for the numerous administrative personnel brought in to support the lesser factotums of the VIP's support staff. The security guard team was more of a paper tiger team in that their appearance and presence although intimidating was backed by very little official authority and the team members were mostly recruited from the ranks of the local unemployed and retired civilians with very little formal security training save for a two day orientation provided by summit organizers. Not very glamorous but necessary and you could bet that me nor my staff would not get any closer to the VIPs than the locals who would watch the black SUV motorcade on the street. My team of guards would be stationed around the outside perimeter and in the common areas frequented not by the VIPs but by the adjunct support staff.

Mine was the assignment that no one really wanted to do, and one that I was never offered but seconded into. When I was briefed on the details of the project I willingly accepted it as I had already finished a grueling project that had seen me manage a forensic investigative team elsewhere in the region and figured that this might just as well be my "decompression" time, especially since the money wasn't all that bad. Besides, in my early (younger) days back home, when my ambition ran well beyond my experience, I would supervise similar security guard teams with Alert Security, Pinkerton's, Wackenhut Corporation and Wells Fargo Security Services. Companies that back in the day gained international acclaim as pioneers and leaders in the North American private contract security industry and of which even to this day, I am proud to have been employed by. These companies had taught me security from the "old school" when getting the job done and results were demanded or you would find yourself unceremoniously unemployed. So, to say the least, I felt that this project was going to be a relatively straightforward endeavor.

I met with the twenty-seven members of my team. A motley crew of men ranging in age from about forty to sixty years. Their state of physical fitness did not leave a great deal to be desired as they were from average to below average when it came to being in shape. It was obvious that these men would definitely not be running anywhere, even if their life depended on it. However, in their uniforms they looked as if they could handle almost any situation. If this was a security enforcement team I would have grave concerns for their safety but in the deployment role our team had, they could easily pull it off. Their physical presence would ensure a certain level of decorum, they could readily communicate any real problems to the security enforcement team and in a real emergency they could act as safety wardens assisting in an evacuation or access control.

After the meeting, I decided to stop in at a local café for a coffee. It didn't take long after I got settled at my table, nursing my coffee when I was approached by the officer designated to be the Field Supervisor on my security team. His appointment as Field Supervisor was the result of a vote held by all of the team members in response to the need to have a single individual be the coordinator of field logistics for the team. Just like the majority of the members of the team, he had no previous law enforcement or military experience but had performed watchman services for about a year at a local factory before it was closed. His previous experience and duties were simply to observe and report incidents, not intervene in or actively apprehend anyone.

The supervisor of my team, Ash as he preferred to be called, voiced concerns about this project and was particularly ill at ease regarding what was expected of the team. For the remainder of about an hour and a half, I reviewed with, and briefed him in greater detail than I had originally presented at the meeting with all the team members in order to reassure him that this mission was an achievable one. The details and reasoning behind the operational methodologies we covered were not really necessary to accomplish the task at hand but gave Ash the personal comfort level he needed to take command of the team. As we discussed these details, the musical radio program that was piped in the café was interrupted with a news report of an incident where some individuals were taken hostage in a neighboring country and the report went on mentioning how politicians were in negotiations with the captors. Ash remarked, that if he was ever taken hostage that he would readily plead for his life with his captors. To me, I personally found this distressing but simply said, "That's not the way I was raised," and left it at that, with Ash having a puzzled look on his face.

All my life, from a part time job as a contract security officer, then my first real fulltime job in a metropolitan police department, to my second fulltime job in the military; my internal programming has been set as a first responder to take command and control of any situation. Even after the military and between jobs, I was active as a volunteer ambulance brigade member which still meant I had to take control when everyone else had lost it. My internal psychological wiring doesn't let me run to the door when things go wrong but rather has me headed in the opposite direction to see what happened and how I can contribute to order in a situation of chaos. As well, I cannot and will not run, back down or bargain with terrorists of any ilk. I only fight battles that I can win; will take calculated risks and act; and have the patience to wait for such an opportunity. I have always credited my Irish grandparents with teaching me how to be civilized in an uncivilized world through the values of honor, duty and service above all else.

We had received a Confidential communiqué from the Intelligence Corps of one of the major nations in attendance that the day before the summit was to begin, a training exercise involving a terrorist hostage incident at one of the hotels that we were assigned to do perimeter security watch was to be staged. Our instructions were on an FYI (For Your Information) only basis as we were not expected to participate in any way. I thought to myself that the scheduling of this training exercise was cutting it pretty close and was wondering how the VIP support staff who had already arrived would take to all this activity. We arrived at the hotel early that morning and I could not help but notice what had appeared to be two RFID (radio frequency identification) pillars just outside a ballroom that was designated for media support staff and government delegate media spokespeople. RFID pillars are those things that most shoppers in the west recognize as the pillars at the exit of a retail store that are supposed to sound an alarm if you walk through them without having the cashier deactivate the RFID tag when paying; an alleged indicator that you may have shoplifted the item. When you walk between these pillars (which are really directional antennas coupled to a transceiver) you are walking through an invisible radio wave field that will activate the tag on an item to send a signal, usually with information regarding the item if the store cashier has not cleared the information on the tag or removed it. Thus alerting store security that you may allegedly be a shoplifter.

I inquired of the hotel manager if he knew why these were here. He told me that some militiamen (local security personnel) had brought these in and told him that they were there to screen for weapons. Of course, I knew that there was no way that these pillars could screen for anything except RFID tags. I located one of the security enforcement officers assigned to patrolling the lobby area, questioned him about these, and he told me the same thing as the manager did; about weapons screening and didn't really seem to care as he yawned and stretched throughout our brief conversation. There was something strange going on here. I sent two of my security men to go back to the hotel I was staying at and bring me, what I called my camera case.

My security men came back, with the larger of the two lugging my black 21" by 14" by 9" PVC Tundra equipment attaché case that easily weighed about 35 lbs. The security man said to me, "What type of camera you got in here anyway?" Of course, when I opened up the case, there was no camera, just electronic instruments. These were the instruments from my previous project that I had to take back home with me. Fortunately, I had a need for them today. The case opening and quick assembly of the equipment was done in a vacant corner of the ballroom just behind the corner of the stage out of eyeshot. Armed with a very small frequency counter and radio frequency field strength/RF power meter, I walked through the pillars nonchalantly as if to just take a look at the adjoining areas.

When I arrived back in the ballroom behind the stage, I glanced down at the frequency counter and it read 13.56 MHz. (Megahertz) and the power output was at 1 watt on the power meter. This really got my mind thinking because the RFID pillars in stores operate between 1.9 to 8.2 MHz., in four specific channels. 13.56 MHz. was definitely not the frequency for this device which meant it had to be specially altered for this frequency. As a matter of fact 13.56 MHz. is the frequency used to activate and read information on access cards and RFID embedded credit cards. However, most RFID card readers for any form of personal identification or access cards use a wall mounted reader where the cardholder must willfully hold their card within 3 inches of it to work. This is because the power output of these readers is typically 90 to 150 mW (milliwatts). It was obvious at this higher output power that these pillars were placed to read the personal information off of anyone's RFID cards as they walked through the pillars right through their wallet or purse, without the individual being any wiser.

With the advent of portable handheld RFID Interrogators (also known as readers) a new trend has begun where organized criminals and terrorists will stand in lines at shopping malls, airports and other public places with a battery powered RFID Interrogator active so that they can obtain information from anyone in the immediate vicinity that has an RFID card with information to provide. RFID Interrogator units can activate and read RFID cards from a distance of 5 inches up to 33 feet away, depending on the output power of the unit. This can easily be done while an RFID card is still in a wallet, purse or pocket. Typically, most of the information on an RFID card is encrypted with 128-bit, Triple DES (Data Encryption Standard) and a one time randomly generated authentication code (especially on credit cards) to reduce identity theft risk. However, despite these measures, scanner software available through underground sources has proven to be capable of retrieving cardholder name, card number and utility data from clandestinely activated (read) RFID cards. Privacy and identity theft risk in this form will only increase as many countries incorporate mandatory RFID microchips in passports, driver's licenses, currency (both paper and coinage), newly redesigned flat (not stamped) nano-technology screened license plates, and RFID micro-tagging of individuals. The use of RFID systems such as these have been discussed and placed under consideration at previous world summits by several national governments and it is only a matter of time before these systems are integrated into the everyday life of the average citizen, with or without their knowledge.

The only defense against this kind of high tech identity theft and privacy invasion is to shield all RFID cards when they are not in use. Back home, many entrepreneuring individuals sell foil or nickel lined wallets and card cases at premium prices to thwart this kind of privacy invasion. However, here on the ground I did not have that luxury or the time for such devices. I ordered two of my men to go to the local hardware store and purchase as many rolls of aluminum foil tape that they could carry; the kind used in plumbing, heating and air conditioning repair. I realized that whoever put that pillar up had the potential of creating a database of personal information off of RFID credit cards, access code information from RFID access cards and would be party to knowing who entered and exited that ballroom in real time! This was something that was not mandated and in my mind took the form of a surreptitious privacy invasion that could create a major incident. Yet no one on the ground seemed to care, to know, or seemed worthy of my trust with regard to this obviously planned clandestine operation.

When my men came back with the boxes of tape, I instructed them to cut lengths of the tape the size of the local paper currency and then to stick the tape on newspapers, and any other freely available paper that they could find. Then I asked them to cut or rip around the tape. They did this for several rolls and looked puzzled but seemed to humor me as they must have thought I had gone totally mad. By the time we were finished we had a few stacks of these aluminum slats. We completed this project just in time, as it appeared that the ballroom was going to be open for the media.

I positioned two of my security guards about 15 feet from the ballroom entrance and the RFID gate. I instructed my men to give every person that intended to enter the ballroom one of the aluminum strips and to instruct them to place it in the bill compartment of their wallet as a security measure. I gave them no other explanation to give to the visitors. For the most part the visitors looked at my security guards as if they were insane but their human nature and curiosity had them complying in any case. This was something I literally banked on. The principle was simple. The aluminum strip when placed in a typical man's wallet would be folded over, enveloping the RFID cards and in turn offering a complete shield that could not be penetrated by the long wavelength frequency used in the pillars. In the case of other wallet styles, the strip would offer some limited protection but I took the gamble that most wallets were of the folded design and that even minimal protection was better than nothing. However, to be really effective the RFID cards should have been sandwiched between two foil plates. A common practice back home by employees at high security installations is to use foil tape on the backs of two of their business cards, cold laminate them and place them in the front and back card compartments of their wallet. This does the job nicely and eliminates the potential of someone reading personal RFID access card data or even RFID credit card information and cloning it for criminal activity, whether it is for identity theft or fraud.

I knew that this little diversion of mine would work because it appeared that the RFID pillars were hooked into what appeared to be the Ethernet wiring in the hotel, which told me the information accessed from the RFID cards of the people walking through the pillars was either being recorded by an automatic (computer) attendant or by an operator who was not in view of the pillars. As well, no one seemed to know how the RFID pillars got there or even wanted to take responsibility for them. Rather than disconnect them or move them, I decided that I wanted to catch the fish that put them there in the first place and even more so, find out why.

As the media people and government press support staff headed towards the ballroom entrance, I quietly laughed to myself watching them all shove aluminum strips into their wallets. Even to this day, there are many reporters that may recall when they were handed a "metal" security pass at a particular summit but still don't know why.

A few hours had passed and fortunately, we didn't run out of aluminum strips. Whoever was monitoring the RFID pillars for data must have been really disappointed at this point. We had heard a large explosion and an announcement was made over a bullhorn that a security exercise had begun. Apart from security teams and militiamen running around the outside of the hotel, it seemed that all was going to be pretty uneventful.

A man dressed in a rather ill kept tan camouflage combat uniform ran through the lobby, with most figuring that this was just part of the security exercise. However, no one was following close behind. I could see him through the open doors of the ballroom, looking quite aggravated. It looked like he was expecting something but whatever it was, it didn't materialize. He then stormed towards the ballroom and shot my two unarmed uniformed security guards that I had posted outside the ballroom entrance. Then once inside the ballroom he waved a 9 mm pistol and ordered everyone to the ground. We all complied and as I looked up slightly I could see that he closed the doors to the ballroom and bolted the doors shut. He then dragged a table to further barricade the doors. Fortunately for me, I was not in a uniform for I am certain that I would not be writing this account. I did have a sidearm (pistol) in a concealment holster in the middle of my lower back and a kubotan on my belt.

A kubotan, developed by and named after Master Takayuki Kubota is a 5.25" long by 0.75" diameter low profile baton (LPB) used primarily as a pain compliance and striking device. For all outward appearances the kubotan just looks like a short stick, very non-threatening and if taken away by an assailant cannot be used against you unless your assailant has been trained in its use; unlike a knife, pepper spray or firearm.

The only thing that would give me away was the metal badge affixed on my belt which I was lying on. He proceeded to yell, that everyone must keep down on the floor. I watched him as he walked out of my normal range of vision but I was able to see his reflection in one of the large mirrored dance balls as he approached a plywood storage chest that was at the foot of the stage. He appeared to have a key for the padlock, where he pulled out a vest with what appeared to have wire connected explosives protruding out of the pockets. I soon realized that he was going to blow-up everyone in the room. I also noted that the explosives were painted blue. Blue paint is used to identify duds or non-working practice pyrotechnic devices for training purposes. I was puzzled but given the circumstances, took this threat seriously. He placed the vest on the stage and stood back as if to admire it and then decided to exercise his bravado in taunting his hostages.

He paced between the bodies of all of us lying on the floor, yelling phrases in his own language, which I could not understand. I decided that I had to act fast if I was to resolve this. In my best estimation there was no rescue team as they were all out on the security exercise and even this incident in progress would have been considered as part of the exercise, even though it wasn't. If this guy had his way, we would all be dead. If I tried and failed, we would all be dead. So, given the options I decided to look for my opportunity. Our captor paced the floor between us, spat on some who were lying on the floor and he even began stomping his steel soled military boot into the backs of the hostages.

I carefully withdrew my kubotan and held it under my body in readiness, waiting for the right moment. He then began walking toward me and he raised his foot to crush my back with his boot and to that I swiftly rolled over and applied the kubotan to his shin before his boot could even come down. He yelled as the kubotan hit the pressure point and he lost his balance. I shouted to everyone to stay down. I had to act fast and countered with a kubotan hold on his left inner wrist to get him to release his weapon. The weapon fell to the ground but with the entire fracas he ended up by the stage lying next to the explosive vest. He stood and looked at me, and said, "It is finished; it is time to die." He then mumbled something in his native language. I picked up his weapon and pointed it at him. We could not have been more than twenty feet apart. He laughed and looked at my badge, noticing that on my leather badge holder was a smaller enameled paramedic qualification badge. He said, "You, you cannot shoot me, you are a healer, you do not know how to take a life. It is against your creed." I asked him to step away from the vest. He declined and I shot him in the knee cap without hesitation, shattering it to which he fell to the ground in excruciating pain. He looked at me, his face tense with the pain he was trying to hide and he said, "You see, you can't even shoot straight, you missed me, I am alive." I said to him, "You're lucky. I am a good shot. I was aiming for your knee." Upon closer careful inspection of the vest it became apparent that it was very much the real thing with deadly explosives wired in parallel and sprayed with blue paint to camouflage their lethal ability.

At that point, a few of the media people unbarricaded the door and ran out to get help. A security enforcement officer rushed in, handcuffed our captor and I ended up tending to his bleeding while awaiting an ambulance despite chastisement from him.

I filed my report with my Project Officer, and later found out at the post debriefing session at the end of the entire project, that the whole security training exercise scheduled that day, to put in my own words was a false flag terror operation. The operation had been staged by one of the nation's intelligence services at the summit to garner support for anti-terror legislation that would ultimately severely erode the rights of their citizens, while increasing financial aid to state corporations. It used unwitting informants with past terrorist group ties at various levels to infiltrate an active militant group and to leak information on the staged security exercise and the placement of the explosive vest. The RFID pillar was placed there to obtain sensitive RFID access card codes, so that they could be cloned and then used by spies to enter security facilities long after the summit had ended. What was even more disturbing was that the RFID pillar was going to be used to announce when a certain press secretary support staffer who had been marked for execution, entered the ballroom by reading his RFID access card, which was a signal for the suicide hostage taker to move in and finish the job.

The staging of false flag terror and organized crime operations is nothing new. Governments have used these operations with unwitting informants and good intentioned accomplices to create a crisis where none existed in order to reaffirm and strengthen their power, politics or financial agenda over the very people who elected them to serve.

▼

CHAPTER 7

Operation Indirect Contact:
THE BACKSTOP AFFAIR

"The world is full of obvious things which nobody by any chance ever observes."

—Sherlock Holmes

In 1995 I had authored a white paper and lectured on custom instructive code (Trojan) viruses that were, and still are virtually undetectable by anti-virus software. This type of computer Trojan virus is capable of searching for specific file names or keywords on an infected computer and then e-mailing the files back to its originator. This instructive code variety or "backstop" as it has been called in the computer underworld defies detection because it is specifically written for its victim and the targeted information it must access.

In order for any anti-virus or computer virus detection software to work, it must be able to recognize the core programming code of the virus it is looking for and then protect against it. This core programming code is often referred to as a virus signature or virus definition. Updated signature or definition files are released as updates on a weekly to bi-weekly basis by most major commercial anti-virus software companies to their subscribers. Approximately five new unique computer viruses are introduced each day and the need to ensure that you have the most updated signatures or definitions for your anti-virus software is critical to the security and privacy of all the information stored on your computer. It must be pointed out that virus signature and definition files can only be generated once a new virus has struck and has been identified. This means that someone, somewhere, perhaps several hundred someones have no doubt encountered a new virus for the first time and have paid the ultimate price—loss of data and privacy. Once reported, virus signature and definition files are updated in order to protect the general computing community. However, "backstop" is a custom engineered instructive code virus and for the most part no two versions are the same. As a result, the "backstop" changes too quickly to be defined, categorized or identified by a static signature. Furthermore, the "backstop" cleans up after itself, removing many tell-tale traces that it even existed once it has executed all of its commands or reached its TTL (Time To Live) date (a pre-programmed time when the instructive code deletes itself).

The "backstop" has the capability to threaten our national security in not less than five ways. 1. Espionage Threat: the "backstop" could be effectively used to identify, target and retrieve information pertaining to our country's national defense. 2. Economic Espionage Threat: the "backstop" could be effectively used to clandestinely identify, target and acquire sensitive financial, trade or economic policy information, proprietary economic information, advanced or innovative technologies, research & development data and proprietary processes and methodologies. 3. National Information Infrastructure Threat: the targeting and clandestine monitoring of computer, cable, satellite, optical and telecommunications systems. 4. Government Systems Threat: the use of the "backstop" in targeting government databases and data communications networks. 5. Foreign Intelligence & Organized Crime Threat: the use of the "backstop" as an intelligence gathering modality in support of an act of espionage, criminal activity or terrorism.

When I identified this new threat, many security gurus and INFOSEC (Information Security) types discounted my concern, with some even offering me their services if I "ever needed a knowledgeable person in INFOSEC." The information (threat) I presented had been based on intelligence that I personally had been privy to, and I offered it to the public domain in a way that would not breach any oath of secrecy I was subject to.

The instructive code or "backstop" searches for specific keywords or phrases. It is delivered to its target as a hidden file attachment piggybacked to an expected attachment, embedded in the body of an e-mail or MP3 file, automatically loaded from a webpage the target is known to frequent, or via external media such as a floppy disk or CD. In one case, the instructive code was delivered on a music CD to an employee known to play music on her laptop. When she connected her laptop to the network, the instructive code transferred itself to its target via the corporate Intranet.

Once on the target system, the code resides in a hidden file that cannot be viewed on the system under regular default settings. The code then searches all files and folders for occurrences of the specific keywords or phrases programmed into it. On a lone computer this is easily accomplished within the time it takes to run an anti-virus scan, while on a network it may take days depending on the size of the network. When matches are found, copies of the data are created, compressed, encrypted and made into a hidden archive file. At a predetermined time, the code automatically e-mails the entire file during a routine e-mail session initiated by the targeted user. Once sent, the code deletes the hidden archive and invokes a self-delete procedure to remove itself, leaving all other files and programs intact. Thus, there is virtually no trace that the instructive code existed on the target system.

Interestingly, it wasn't until four years later that a spokesperson of a major federal intelligence agency was cited in a small filler article carried through the American Press News syndicate that he felt instructive code viruses may pose a national security risk. Of course, it is a matter of public record that my white paper on the "backstop" identified this risk in 1995.

Due to the very nature and purpose of instructive code Trojans, it is unlikely that victim statistics will truly reflect the real financial impact the backstop will have in the corporate sector, or on national and international security. As with any act of espionage, typically only 3% of incidents globally ever get reported for fear of repercussions of corporate non-competence and weakened government diplomatic relations. The slightest hint of an espionage incident in the competitive corporate sector can adversely affect share prices, consumer confidence, deteriorate market share and can draw focus on legislated external industry regulation in industries that prefer self-regulation. It is these factors that cause most corporations not to report such incidents to public law enforcement nor seek criminal prosecution for perpetrators but rather conduct their own internal investigations leading to civil litigation against perpetrators. It has been estimated that not more than 20% of reported corporate espionage cases worldwide result in criminal conviction.

After doing a local radio talk show on privacy and technology, I received an e-mail from a listener that was concerned about his privacy. Usually when I do any kind of guest appearance whether it be on local radio or national television, as a courtesy the host will make my website available to the audience for follow-up information. This is one of the reasons I make an extra effort to ensure that all material on my website is up-to-date and easy to understand for non-technical people. As media appearances, conferences and lectures currently take up about half of my forensic practice activities, I get hundreds of e-mails daily from people wanting me to help them with their specific situation. In most cases I respond back to them with an appropriate contact in their area who can work with them on what they need worked out or for the follow-up information they require. However, this e-mail piqued my interest.

The e-mail in question related the story of a gentleman who worked in the research and development department of an industrial technology firm. Apparently the man, on his own time and in his basement workshop developed a revolutionary imaging compression system and the multi-national corporation whom he was employed by for several years wanted the rights to it. This intrigued me and I decided to meet the man in a local downtown café to discuss his situation.

The next day we met at my favorite café in the downtown Days Inn just two blocks from police headquarters and four blocks from the forensic science center; two of my regular stops whenever I make my rounds downtown. Graham was in his mid-40's and had curly medium brown hair that was only subdued by traces of male pattern baldness. His personality seemed very conservative and he spoke only after giving thought to what he would say, and then delivered it in short, sharp sentences. As he spoke his eyes often looked around the café as if he were looking for someone or something. He told me how he developed software that had the capability of compressing extremely high resolution digital images to easily thirty percent less of what the best image format can do today. What this meant was that using his new technology, higher resolution images could be stored, transmit or viewed over the Internet at twice the speed and take up less space. This also meant better graphics capability all around for online applications and software.

The company he worked for was not in the graphics business but in the area of software for controlling heavy industrial equipment. He was quick to point out that his employer was not involved in the area of technology which his own personal research project was based and that he never used his employer's equipment to do any work on this project. Yet, he had been approached on not less than three occasions by a certain Mr. Young from corporate head office located just over 600 miles from the subsidiary that employed him, in an attempt to learn more about his research, its final prototype and an offer to buy the rights to it for $56,000. Graham declined, mostly due to the fact that he felt that his research and prototype was far from being truly developed to the level he felt that it could be. However, what really got him concerned was the manner in which he had been approached and the circumstances surrounding the entire incident.

Graham told me constantly and insistently throughout our conversation, that he never used his firm's equipment to do his personal project and he never did any work on it at his place of employment, let alone mention it to anyone. Even more odd was that Mr. Young of corporate head office told Graham that the company's offers and negotiations with him, even the fact that he was contacted at all was confidential and that under the existing Non-Disclosure Agreement he signed as part of the terms and conditions of his employment that he could not discuss any of this with anyone, including managers and executives at his workplace. What really got Graham concerned enough to contact me was the nagging question of how the corporate head office knew of his project.

It is a given in today's high technology based competitive corporate environments that 68% of employers monitor and review the e-mails, voice-mails and company computer generated documents of their employees. This monitoring and review is only legally exercised in the office and on company owned or leased equipment and services such as a company mobile telephone, e-mail or voice mail accounts that could be accessed outside of the physical office. Graham used none of these to pursue his research activity.

Graham's situation struck me as a very odd one indeed. After about two hours of being briefed on his unusual and personally unsettling situation, I decided to offer my assistance. A primary concern of Graham's was that if someone knew of his research, what else did they or could they know of, or have access to when it came to his personal life and its associated activities.

My first step was to conduct a thorough sweep for electronic surveillance devices (hidden cameras, microphones, tracking transmitters and telephone monitoring devices) in Graham's home and in his two automobiles. The sweep came up negative—absolutely nothing found. I then decided to focus my attention on Mr. Young of the corporate head office. In calling the telephone number Graham had for Mr. Young after hours, I received a very business like voice mail message, just as one would expect. I then decided to press the "0" button on my telephone to connect to reception or the general delivery voice mailbox as is usually the case on most mid-to-large telephone systems. However, this gave me a voice prompt that stated the command was invalid. This got me curious, so I ran a check on the telephone number and it came back as a cellular telephone number. I then called the corporate head office main telephone number, and being that it was after hours I knew that I would get the automated attendant (voice mail) system. At the prompt, I pressed the octothorpe (pound #) symbol and entered the staff directory. I entered our Mr. Young's name and it returned the extension of only one Mr. Young. I proceeded to connect to his extension at which point I was greeted by the message, "this is Dave Young of building maintenance, please leave a message." This was even more of a puzzle. I managed to record Mr. Young's voicemail greeting and would ask Graham if this voice sounded like his Mr. Young.

The next day I replayed the voicemail message, purposely excluding the reference to building maintenance for Graham, at which point he immediately identified the voice. From that moment my inquiries became focused on Mr. Young. Through extensive database searches it appeared that Mr. Young had been employed at the corporate head office for about 3 years in the building maintenance department, and prior to that he was a full time university student for 2 years, enrolled in an eclectic collection of computer programming courses with no degree specified as a final goal. Before entering university, he was a student in his native China.

It has been established by several Western intelligence agencies that China has sent approximately 600,000 students during the period 1980 to 2005 into the west, as part of its national policy of developing an innovative science and technology infrastructure for the future. Many of these students are sponsored by the Chinese government and her national corporations, and one may readily assume in a culture where there is a less legalistic view of copyrights, patents, trademarks and intellectual property in general, that the pursuit of gathering commercial or military information for the benefit of one's nation is not considered out of bounds. From 1985 to 2005, foreign nationals of South Korea, Taiwan, Philippines, Israel, Greece, Saudi Arabia, Iraq, Jordan, Ghana, Liberia, South Africa, El Salvador, Ecuador, Russia, China, Pakistan, India and France have been identified and investigated for espionage in the west in relation to the acquisition of host nation intelligence data or intellectual property.

It was apparent that Mr. Young was not acting on behalf of corporate head office but on behalf of another entity. Given Mr. Young's background in computer programming, I turned my attention to Graham's computers in his home. I conducted an extensive examination of the contents of Graham's hard drive but found nothing that appeared unusual. However, I came across a rather odd Children's educational program on his computer that installed some sort of program on the hard drive but required that the CD be placed in the CD drive in order to run the program. I asked Graham where he had obtained the program. He told me that it was a free program, available in the information rack in the lobby at his workplace. This got me curious, so I made a copy of his CD and took it back to my laboratory for more in-depth analysis. It took me about a day and a half of reverse engineering to realize that this was a "backstop" program that had a key word list of about 100 targeted words. Once this program was installed on a computer, it would look for word processing, spreadsheet and presentation documents that incorporated any one of the 100 targeted words while the user would be using the Children's educational program, and then e-mail a copy of the documents to its originator whenever the computer was online. The destination e-mail address was a free Internet e-mail account which had more than likely been registered using fictitious personal information.

Knowing what to look for in the program, I arranged to obtain a few of these CDs from the information rack at his workplace to determine if the "backstop" was present in all of them or just on Graham's copy. After my examination of these free CDs, it became evident that the same instructive code Trojan was on them as well. With the help of some associates, we canvassed other buildings in the neighborhood and soon discovered that these CDs were placed in several information racks in various lobbies and reception areas throughout the business park. The business park catered to industrial and heavy engineering type operations that designed, modified or assembled equipment.

Realizing the threat posed by this, and the unknown number of infected computers with this "backstop" program, my associates and I worked on creating a small removal program that could thoroughly and safely remove the "backstop." We immediately released this information to the anti-virus software community and posted our removal program as a free download on our websites. Realizing that it would take time for all this to make it to the untold number of infected computer users, we did this as soon as we could to get the ball rolling, while in this ramp up period, I focused my attention on Mr. Young. Through my contacts I was able to obtain information on the ISP (Internet Service Provider) that had been used to access the free e-mail address used to receive the stolen data file copies made by the "backstop." Although the log indicated access from three different IP Addresses at different times of the day, I went with the most frequented IP Address that coincidentally seemed to be used between 8:00 pm and 3:00 am. The IP Address identified the Internet Service Provider and in making "official" enquiries, I was able to associate the IP Address to a specific cable modem, and subscriber. The subscriber was none other than Mr. Young.

The IP Address, also referred to as an Internet address is a unique 32-bit address represented as four octets separated in dotted decimal format. To the lay person, an IP Address can be likened to a unique digital serial number that looks like nnn.nnn.nnn.nnn, where "n" represents a number. Every ISP (Internet Service Provider) has blocks or groups of these numbers that are registered to them for their exclusive use. Whenever one of their users (subscribers) accesses the Internet, they do so with an IP Address allocated by their ISP. For users that use a modem and telephone line (also known as dial-up Internet), an IP Address is typically assigned at random from a pool of addresses for that particular session (connection) and then when the user logs off, the IP Address is released back into the pool and then reassigned to another user who dials in. However, high speed Internet subscribers, such as those who use cable, DSL or any other "always on" Internet connection methodologies are assigned a permanent IP Address from their ISP for as long as they remain a subscriber of that particular ISP. This makes the tracking of the users' activity and their identification much easier.

At this point, my function as an investigator was over and the next step was to hand the evidence I had and case file to federal law enforcement authorities in order to take the matter to the next level. As far as the initial purpose of my engagement on Graham's behalf, I was able to address his original concern of privacy by identifying the problem and solving it. In doing so, we uncovered a more sinister operation. I also contacted the I.T. (Information Technology) Manager of Graham's employer and provided him with the "backstop" removal software my team developed.

It was about a month later that I had been told "unofficially" by an associate of mine that Mr. Young who allegedly wrote this "backstop" version had the program hidden in a Children's Educational Program, a CD/DVD Duplication Program and a Pop-Up Killer Program. He had each of the three programs professionally duplicated and packaged in CD format, complete with attractive packaging. These programs were offered for free to unsuspecting users, mostly employees at technology based firms, via free information racks or left on reception desks. Knowing that most would give this free, legitimate looking software a try at least once, he was able to infect the computers of technology staff with his "backstop" in order to recover sensitive personal data and company proprietary information. The information obtained was provided to offshore contacts for the purposes of intellectual property infringement and identity theft. While his employment as a maintenance worker covered his living expenses, his computer CD business had been subsidized by third party transfers to his bank account. A spot audit of his e-mails revealed that his software had been monitoring no less than 3,500 different computer users. As a result of the federal investigation into his activities, Mr. Young was arrested and convicted of espionage under the U.S. Economic Espionage Act.

CHAPTER 8

▼

Operation Ulterior:
THE TAKE-AWAY AFFAIR

"You are suspicious of me because I am different. I am suspicious of you because you are all the same."

—Anon

It was springtime in Gloucester and although we had a relatively mild winter, the 65 degree weather in mid-May was a welcome sign from the dull, often near freezing days of the previous month. The city had changed considerably over the years with an influx of immigrants from South Asia. Walking down the main street you could easily pick-up the scent of South Asian cuisine from the handful of small shops that were sporadically placed between other more traditional North American stores. It was this new eclectic blend of cultures that brought new money and growth to what once was a sleepy bedroom community for commuters to the capital.

Over the years, I had gotten to know many of the proprietors of these shops, as my adventure for trying new foods always found me asking them what it was that I just ate; long after the fact, and on some occasions at great peril to my digestive system! It was on such an occasion when I found myself at a South Asian fast food counter in a small ten foot by fifteen foot shop. This was literally just a take out counter with no seating. Here you would order your food, receive it in a brown paper bag, pay and go. Cash only. Despite the spartan look of this place, the food was good and had quite a customer base in the neighborhood. It was obvious that the overhead was low and the demand was high, so this little business was really doing well. I recall at lunch time, some days it did so well that customers would be lined up from the counter all the way into the street, with a line of at least ten people or more.

The proprietor Raj, was well liked and well known by everyone in the neighborhood. During the really cold winter months he would always have a pot of hot coffee or hot chocolate for what he called the "wanderers." The wanderers of course were the street people, the homeless who could always get a free hot drink from Raj on a blistery night.

Today I had a taste for hoppers with lunu miris and was fortunate to get into the shop about an hour past the lunchtime rush with only one other customer in the shop ahead of me. The young girl behind the counter took my order, and Raj just happened to peer out from behind the kitchen door. At that point he approached me and asked if he could see me after the shop closed as he had a business matter to discuss. Raj knew that I was involved in the security field but I didn't think he knew much more about me. In our brief exchange, I agreed to come back to the shop after closing to meet with him. I agreed to this more out of my own curiosity than anything else.

Later that evening I arrived at Raj's shop and knocked on the locked door several times, but did not get a response. Figuring that Raj must have forgotten or just changed his mind, I headed toward my car. At that point Raj pulled up in his car and motioned me to get in. I obliged, not knowing what I was in for. During the 3 minute drive to our destination; a nearby shopping mall parking lot, Raj said nothing and I found myself, for whatever reason, not saying anything either. He pulled into one of the parking stalls, turned the lights and engine off. At this point my defensive instincts were running scenarios in my mind.

He turned to me and said, "Mr. Robert, I have had you as a customer in my shop for the past several years. I need your advice, but you must not say anything to anyone, about what I will tell you." At this point Raj stared straight into my eyes with his steely black eyes highlighted only by the white of his own bloodshot sclera. I assured him that I would listen to what he wanted to tell me and maintain his confidentiality.

He told me that a former schoolmate, Saamy, from back home, now a refugee in this country and re-united close friend of his here, whom he had known for the past year informed him that two illegals from back home had been hired to kill him. The illegals living here under fraudulent identities had apparently shown Saamy photographs of Raj's daughter, currently in her first year residence at an American university on a student visa. Saamy continued to explain that if these two illegals could not kill Raj, they would easily have his daughter killed in place of him. Raj was told by Saamy that luckily, these individuals had been ordered not to carry out the killing of him or his daughter if an amount of US$50,000 in cash deposited into an offshore bank account in Antigua by the end of the month.

Raj explained that he was no one of importance back home or even here in his new country, and that he could not understand why someone would want to do such a thing. He turned to me and merely wanted to solicit from me an opinion and from what I sensed, a positive affirmation that he should pay the money. I was at a loss to offer either. I asked him if he thought about going to the police and telling them about this. He flatly refused and said, "This is not our way. This is our community and what happens in our community, stays in our community. I do not trust these police, they are for westerners here." He seemed quite adamant about this position, yet I was puzzled as to why he chose me to get a second opinion on this. I did not venture to ask as I did not want to risk closing the line of communication with him. I asked Raj if he could give me the banking details and tell me about his early days back home in the hopes that he would unknowingly tell me more about his friend Saamy. It is a given in the art and science of intelligence, that if you ask direct questions that the responses may not be 100% accurate, but if you strike up a conversation on a topic and carefully steer the subject matter to what you are interested in; the information that is volunteered will be much more reliable. I did this with Raj and our conversation ended with much more information on Saamy than I could have come across from hours of research elsewhere.

The next day I began my enquiries with a focus on the offshore bank in Antigua. While most people think of Swiss banks as the best place to anonymously hide money; with the amount of anti-money laundering and tax legislation over the past ten years, Swiss banks are not quite as lucrative for criminal activity as they used to be. This being the case; offshore banks in the former Soviet Union, the Caribbean and South America have been established to re-work old loopholes. Add to this the capability of opening and maintaining an account online via the Internet, and things move much faster with even less of a paper trail and physical presence than before. For the criminal, this has been a definite advantage from both sides of the virtual teller's cage. This particular offshore bank in Antigua as I began to learn was exactly this.

The bank in question went by the name ALT Union Trust and was based on the tiny island of Antigua. ALT had an impressive, very professional designed website that utilized a secure connection the minute you opened the bank's welcome page as witnessed by the little padlock icon in the web browser's lower right toolbar. Even major North American banks don't greet you with such a secure connection on their opening welcome page! The graphics and flash animations of happy bank customers and staff gave the impression that no expense was spared in serving customers, and that you too could join the elite client list of this bank at the click of a mouse. The bank offered savings, checking and investment accounts. As well, an array of popular secured major name credit cards was on offer. A regular major name credit card could be had for an account with an opening balance of US$5,000; a gold card for US$12,000; and a platinum card for US$25,000 with absolutely no credit check and issued in anyone's name you would like; perhaps even your pet budgie if you felt "Polly" deserved it. Of course this was all too overwhelming in just one visit, so I ended up making several visits to the site to learn as much as I could about how ALT operated. On my last visit to the website I soon came to the realization that this bank was definitely targeting Western consumers who wanted a private alternative solution to traditional national banks, and if the bank couldn't get consumers to bite on this, they upped the ante by offering 23 percent interest rates on their own branded "guaranteed" deposit certificates, while the traditional banks back home offered rates of up to 8 percent at the time. Most investors would probably ask themselves if this rate were too good to be true and follow-up with checking if the bank was chartered or insured. However, the bank literally "banked" that most general consumers would accept whatever was published on their website.

Having all the information I needed from the bank's perspective, I then started my enquiries from a more traditional perspective. I soon learned that client deposits were in no way insured, nor was this bank chartered or in any way recognized by the U.S. Federal Deposit Insurance Corporation or Canada Deposit Insurance Corporation. I began to call some of my associates who were employed in various investigative roles throughout three levels of government in order to see if I could get an opinion or "a word on the street" about this bank.

I obtained confirmation from several sources that this bank was nothing but an online scam, set up to bilk unsuspecting depositors of their money. It was believed that the bank during its operation of just under a year had acquired from depositors close to US$12 million. Normally, with most online fraudulent banks the story would end at this point and when it comes to fraudulent online banking it is believed that fraudulent banks typically make up about 8% of online banking websites worldwide.

However, I was advised by one of my sources that the bank was alleged to be linked to a South Asian terrorist and organized crime group. The proceeds were allegedly being used to fund criminal activities in the region. This operation posed a double threat from a national security perspective as it not only obtained money to fund terrorist and organized crime operations but also obtained personal identification information such as social security numbers, dates of birth, employment, credit and family information from unsuspecting clients that could readily be used by known terrorists to impersonate law abiding citizens to gain employment, credit or travel documents anywhere in the world.

Today, identity theft is no longer carried out by criminals solely as an aid to financial fraud but is also used by terrorists and organized criminals to gain access to borders, employment and "an ordinary life" in an ordinary community until it is time for them to execute their plan. A complete stolen identity information package including social security number, date of birth, driver's license number, immediate genealogy, credit report and resume can sell for as little as $100 or $800 with forged or replacement government issued identification documents.

While there are legitimate banks that operate online banking operations for their customers, consumers must be very cautious to ensure that the bank they are dealing with is a bona fide, legal institution that will not steal their money or their identity. If a bank offers an extraordinary rate of interest on deposits, does not have a physical street address with a telephone number listed on its website (not a post office box), does not have its bank name as the domain name (i.e. www.thisbank.com) or the name does not appear in the upper left hand corner of your Internet browser's window; you should be very suspicious. You can further check the bank out by contacting your local Federal Deposit Insurance Corporation office in the U.S. or the Canada Deposit Insurance Corporation in Canada.

While authorities were coordinating an effort to shut this operation down, they were still conducting monitoring and surveillance in order to ensure they had all the evidence they needed to apprehend and convict all concerned. I was given the impression that this "online bank" would be shut down within the next 60 days but this was only based on my own deductive reasoning.

Knowing this told me that the money Raj was to deposit in this bank would allegedly be used for terrorist or organized criminal activity back in his native country. Now that I figured what the money might be used for, next on my list was Raj's friend Saamy. It didn't take long to run Saamy's name through several databases and notice that he always seemed to be within arms length of certain individuals suspected of organized criminal activity. I placed a call to an associate of mine involved in performing security clearance checks. He advised me that Saamy was considered a "pointer person." A "pointer person" is a term used in some intelligence circles to identify a person who may not directly or indirectly be involved in a criminal activity but is known to associate with someone who is, and therefore, if you ever have to find that "someone", you execute surveillance on the "pointer person" who will point you in their direction. My security clearance operator put me in contact with an "old clothes" investigator that worked in the South Asian community.

The term "old clothes" refers to an investigator that wears common street clothes to enable him to blend in, but unlike an undercover investigator, some key people in the community know that he is an investigator and he will readily intervene in a life and death situation, while clearly identifying himself as such. An undercover investigator involved in intelligence work will never divulge his identity. Just as an aside, a "plain clothes" investigator is your typical detective with a clean shirt, optional tie and bulky jacket or overcoat to conceal the equipment (radio, handcuffs, weapon, etc.) on his belt.

The "old clothes" investigator had told me the word on the street was that Saamy was planning a trip back home and he was trying to make a name for himself by raising money for organized criminal activities back home by persuading members of the local ethnic community here to contribute large sums of money. The contact also told me that no one on the organized criminal side took Saamy seriously and that they just used him. It was obvious that there was no logical reason why a contract to kill Raj or his daughter had been put in place. The contract was a fabrication on the part of Saamy to attempt to extort money from Raj, a friend from the past, in order to bolster Saamy's standing with his criminal associates.

Armed with this information, but realizing how sensitive and distrusting Raj was of the authorities, I decided to execute a plan that would keep everyone happy and apprehend Saamy. I contacted some associates of mine involved in the intelligence community and those involved in the investigation of ALT Union Trust. Physical and electronic surveillance was to be focused on Raj's and Saamy's place of business. Being that this matter involved terrorism and national security issues, the securing of legal authorization to covertly place physical and electronic surveillance on both these locations was fast tracked and given the "green light."

I instructed Raj to go through with the deal with Saamy but to tell him that he would have to personally guide him on how to do this financial transaction on the computer. Raj and Saamy arranged to meet that night and unbeknownst to either one of them, the ALT Union Trust site had been shut down and what they would logon to would be a "spoofed" (a reasonable facsimile) of the original site that was specially set up on a local law enforcement agency computer network.

Spoofing is a computer security term that refers to making a complete recreation of a legitimate website so that it looks and acts exactly like the original but is actually under the control of someone else and is hosted on another server (computer network). Crackers (criminal hackers) typically will spoof (copy) legitimate bank and e-commerce websites in order to lure consumers to enter their account and credit information so that they (the Crackers) may either use the credit information fraudulently or resell the information to other third parties for criminal activity. Most people are lured to the spoofed websites by receiving an e-mail allegedly from their financial institution or a retailer they have done business with, requesting that they click on a link in the e-mail and answer a few questions to verify their identity in order to keep their account active.

Some spoofers may even go so far as having the e-mail link take the recipient to a legitimate website but will also run a special script program that will cause a "fake" logon pop-up window to appear over the legitimate site asking for personal information in order to continue; which when completed is sent directly to the cracker, and the recipient is just left looking at the legitimate website. The best defense against being a victim of spoofing is to never click on a link in an e-mail; even if it looks like it is from an institution or retailer you have an account with. Rather, if you think there is a chance it is legitimate, telephone the accounts department of your institution or retailer but don't click on the link. In our case, we spoofed the website and we were also able to take control of the domain name used by ALT Union Trust in order to redirect it to our secure server so that we could apprehend Saamy in the commission of the crime.

Every keystroke, every conversation during the event was logged. Raj asked Saamy several times if he and his daughter would be safe after paying this money, and Saamy confirmed this, and proved he knew all the workings of this online fraud and extortion scheme.

Once the deal had been completed, Saamy left Raj's shop, and was apprehended a few blocks away. Saamy was charged and convicted of funding terrorist activities, extortion and bank fraud. Further questioning and investigation of Saamy revealed that other members of the local South Asian community had been victims of Saamy's extortion schemes. Raj never lost a penny out of his bank account and although suspicious as to how everything worked out, he still considers himself to be a man of few questions, content with working in his shop and living in his little community.

CHAPTER 9

▼

Operation Intervene:
THE PIXEL AFFAIR

*"The absence of existence exists and therefore reality consists of
complete subjectivity."*

—Anon

I received a telephone call from an associate who was in charge
of internal security for a major corporation. With new, tougher
legislated guidelines on how corporations collect, use, disclose
and dispose of information gathered in the course of their
commercial activity, he wanted to have an independent third
party observer to ensure corporate due diligence in the deletion
of computer data files. He asked if I would be interested, and
although this was really not the type of engagement I would
normally consider, I accepted the project given that we had
served on a couple of overseas assignments together and we both
shared a professional respect for each other.

I arrived at the corporate technology center the following
morning. The technology center was where all decommissioned
company computers and other devices were sent from field

offices across the country to meet their final fate. That fate would be one of three things: being resold to a surplus liquidator, being donated to a charity or being sent to the scrap heap. My job was simply to observe that the hard drives of the computers had been forensically wiped of all client and employee data, and to test and verify that this was done successfully. Thus ensuring that critical data such as health records, credit and employee information could not be recovered from any of the decommissioned computers no matter where they ultimately ended up; from curbside dumpster to second hand shop. The process was carried out with assembly line efficiency and it didn't take long for the team to make a dent in the 250 decommissioned machines.

As part of the process I would actually attempt to access random data on the computer drives just to ensure that all had been unrecoverably deleted. While doing this double check, I found myself in front of employee workstation ID Tag # 31109-B-021. It was there that I located a lone encapsulated postscript (eps) graphics file. This seemed odd, to find a graphics file on a workstation that was tasked with processing text only files. I copied the graphics file onto a disk and opened the file in my iPhoto Plus program and was shocked to find a semi-clad African girl of no more than 12 years of age, just standing in the photograph, with a woeful look in her eyes, surrounded by what looked like the décor of a half star motel. I asked my associate about the computer workstation and the photo, and he gave me an apprehensive look as he related the story of Workstation 31109-B-021. Apparently about 18 months before the workstation found its way to the technology center it was used for over 6 years by an employee who had been subsequently arrested, charged and convicted under Child

Pornography legislation. Under a dragnet operation aimed at apprehending distributors and recipients of Child Pornography, a special multi-agency law enforcement team operating under the code name Project "P" maintained an extensive months long vigilance in tracking Child Pornographers. Mr. M, the company employee assigned to this workstation had been allegedly found receiving and redistributing pornographic images of children.

My associate told me that Workstation 31109-B-021 had been seized by federal agents and had been retained by them for approximately 6 months after which it had been released back to the corporation with what appeared to be all illegal images removed. However, it did appear that this one image seemed to slip by. Although to an untrained observer the photograph could have been taken on vacation by a parent or guardian, the look in the eyes of the subject and surroundings eerily gave a different message.

I recalled hearing and reading about the multiple arrests made by the multi-agency task force through the media. It was certainly a major victory on the ground for all concerned. Of course the politicians got their air time and promised that legislation would be forthcoming to ensure that our communities would be protected against child pornography by mandating filtering software be utilized by every Internet Service Provider within the Nation and at the first sign of child pornography, to enforce a denial of service policy to shut out the offenders. From the law enforcement side, this meant the apprehension of distributors and recipients as usual and if at all possible the identification of the victimized children involved. Of course, most of this activity would be used to clean up this abomination in our own backyard and save those innocents within our western borders. However, it is my feeling that when it comes to child pornography, we must understand that we cannot afford to believe that because we have insulated ourselves from it in our part of the world by filtering, saving our own children and apprehending the miscreants in our manor that we have actually made headway into ending it globally or deterring the pornographic wolves beyond the walls of our filtered western fortress. To me, the real solution is to aggressively seek out the manufacturers and producers of child pornography no matter where they may be on this earth. We have the technology and could commit the resources, but the political will of most nations is not there to accomplish such a task. Having said this, I want to make it clear that I respect and do recognize the work of law enforcement in this area and given their limited resources, they have done nothing short of miracles on a daily basis in the areas of apprehension and rescue in cases of alleged child pornography but they need more. I started a personal project called the "Ing Initiative" the details of which can be found in Appendix B. I urge readers to support law enforcement in their activities regarding child pornography and to let their politicians know of their support.

After hearing about the details surrounding Workstation 31109-B-021, the image of the little girl impacted me even more. Although I had no doubt that the authorities used all resources available to investigate the situation, the forensic investigator in me would not let go of this lone piece of evidence or the image of innocence lost so easily. I asked if I could analyze the graphics file in order to attempt to trace its origin. I was given permission to do so with the condition that I would not remove the image file from the premises.

The following day I returned to the corporate technology center armed with digital forensic software and analysis equipment. After running a battery of rigorous digital forensic analysis on the image, I had been able to recover an electronic serial number of the actual digital camera that had been used to take the image. Most current higher end digital camera models embed a unique electronic serial number in the actual image that they create. This unique serial number identifies the camera manufacturer, model and the exact camera used. As well, I was successful in retrieving information on the software used to edit the image. This information included the name and manufacturer of the software, its version number and product serial key. Having retrieved all of this information would enable me to hopefully reverse engineer the image from an investigative standpoint and ultimately track down where the image came from and perhaps locate who created it.

Back at my own lab, I used my resources to decode the electronic serial number which identified the make and model of the camera used. From the model of the camera, I learned that this particular model was a European version, only distributed and sold in European markets. I contacted the warranty registration department of the manufacturer in Hamburg, Germany in an attempt to retrieve the name and address of the registered owner of the camera, based on the serial number. My efforts were met with great opposition and a complete lack of cooperation from the warranty service manager, as while she confirmed that the information was on file, she was not at liberty to divulge or cooperate with my inquiry as I had no legal authority in the execution of my request. Undaunted by this, I turned my attention on the information I obtained pertaining to the graphics software.

From the software manufacturer's website, I discovered that the software version used to edit the image; version 5.5 had been replaced by version 6.0 and then version 7.2. Not wanting to make the same mistake twice, being that I was merely some "Joe Bloggins" in this whole scenario acting on absolutely no authority from any government agency, I decided to try a different approach in my inquiry with the software company. I contacted the customer service department of the software company in Berkeley, California via their toll free telephone number. After about 15 minutes of being placed on hold by an automated system, repeatedly telling me in a synthesized female voice how my call was important between snippets of extremely bad generic versions of pop music, my call was answered by a real person.

Many years ago, when computers were first introduced to the small and medium sized business markets, they were touted as giving both employees and employers the ability to get more work done in less time, meaning greater productivity and faster solutions to problems. This new technology was sold to the masses as having the potential of giving employees shorter work weeks, giving clients improved customer service levels and reducing overhead costs for business owners. Business operators soon realized that they could do more work in less time but kept the working hours of employees pretty much the same, and in some industries turned their weekday 9–5 operation to a 7 day a week, 24-hour operation at the peril of an underpaid, over-extended work force. In the interest of improved customer service delivered at a lower cost, customer service staff these days, are on average at 30% of staffing levels than what they were ten years ago. Clients are typically handled by automated systems on a self-serve (fend-for-yourself) basis that provide "canned" cookie cutter service that typically addresses the needs and wants of the 70% of the customer base who have been conditioned to the customer service credo, "If you want us to serve you, you better take the time to navigate our telephone or website menu first and then we will permit you to serve yourself because you are important to us." To add insult to injury at the expense of real customer service, most customer service representatives in call centers only earn wages to a maximum of 25% of the legislated minimum hourly wage rate. I intended to use this situation completely to my advantage.

The customer service representative introduced herself as Jill. I told Jill that my ex-brother-in-law gave me this software for Christmas some years ago and that he registered it for me. Now, despite having been unhappily divorced from his sister, I told Jill, that I was trying to piece my life back together as a professional photographer and wanted to upgrade this software so I could get my small business on track. I wanted to pay for the upgrade versus the full version price but did not know what my ex-brother-in-law registered my software under. Jill was sympathetic to my plight and asked me if I had the original software CD with the product serial key on it. Of course, I didn't but as I had the product serial key, I could fake it and tell her I did. Working off the premise that there was no way that I would know the 18 digit alpha-numeric serial key unless I had the original CD, she checked the status of "my" software on the company database after I read it to her. She told me that the registration was still good and that I could upgrade online over the company website. I cautiously asked what information I needed to do this on the website. She gave me a rather lengthy website address and told me that all that I had to do was enter my product serial key and my software version and the online wizard would do the rest. When I heard this I knew that automated customer service would not fail me. I thanked Jill and armed with the website address I was ready to go to take my quest to the next level.

Logging in from my laptop using a dial-up connection to the website was child's play. I was greeted by a screen asking for my product serial key and software version number. I carefully typed these in and hit the enter button. It was there, on the next screen that I was greeted by the usual promotional graphics proclaiming the greatness of the latest software version but of more interest were the menu tabs across the top of the screen which read, "News, Account Manager, Upgrade, Products and Contact Us." Of course, the specific menu tab of interest was "Account Manager." I clicked on there and was greeted with a screen that had an online form with the fields, "Company Name, Contact Person, E-mail, Address, City, State, Zip, Country, Telephone and Webpage." What made this more interesting was that all of the information was filled in! I proceeded to print out the page and save a screen shot of it on my computer. At the bottom of this form were the buttons, "Edit, Delete, Cancel, Save and OK." I clicked OK and exited the website.

From the registrant information, I had the registered owner of the software being a Diettmarr E., with a company called XNV Commerce located on Boulevard de LaMarina in Cotonou, Benin. Using my available online database resources I ran a check on Diettmarr and his company XNV Commerce. I was also able to pull his e-mail address off of the registration information which led to a free e-mail service provided by a North Korean ISP (Internet Service Provider) that had been shut down due to the hosting of fraudulent and pornographic websites within the past few months. The business registration information I was able to obtain indicated that XNV Commerce was an import—export wholesale company operating throughout West Africa with its home base in Cotonou. Intelligence records information on Diettmarr indicated that he had been under investigation on several occasions regarding allegations of kidnapping and slave trading. However, he had never been convicted in any court of law over the span of the 12 years that the allegations had covered.

In the weeks that followed my Internet research and network of associates had provided me an introduction to, and contact with an investigator of an international aid agency operating in West Africa. The investigator, Bill, a former aid worker was responsible for reporting and documenting human rights violations in the region and briefing his agency employer in Geneva. After several e-mail and telephone communiqués with Bill, I had soon realized that West Africa had an extremely high incidence of child slave trafficking. That this activity was quite common in Benin, Burkina Faso, Cameroon, Cote d'Ivoire, Nigeria and Togo.

Bill had told me that culturally, the responsibility for educating children in persistently impoverished Africa had been delegated to an extended family system. It was not uncommon for middle or senior aged "Sugar Daddies" or "Rich Uncles" to provide young girls with money for education, books, clothes, or family support in exchange for domestic help. However, with economic pressures and persistent poverty many girls had found themselves sold into commercial labor mills or even worse, into sexual exploitation. The average age ranges for female child slaves was between 6 to 16, but Bill was quick to point out that even infants of barely a few months old and older teenage girls were also being sold and traded.

Diettmarr was a known operator in the region to Bill. Bill had confided that Diettmarr's name had been on several incident reports alleging him as the primary perpetrator or instigator of buying, selling and trading children for labor camps and sexual exploitation. Brokers such as Diettmarr would scout for children amongst poor families in rural areas throughout West African countries. The brokers would routinely spend days rounding up children, crossing borders with a cavalier laissez-faire attitude. When finding a child they wanted, they would approach the parents with the offer that they represented a wealthy family or they were respected businessmen and that they would adopt or sponsor the child, ensuring that the child would receive professional training, a university education and be well looked after in exchange for the child performing basic domestic duties at their home abroad. The parents of these children, most often illiterate themselves, not world wise, but wishing the best opportunity for their child, and tempted by the cash offer made by the broker would find the arrangement hard to resist. Those parents who would resist might find that their child had gone missing very shortly, as some brokers readily kidnapped any child they set their mind on. As for the amount of cash that would be offered to buy a child from their parents in West Africa; Bill told me the going rate averaged from US$15 to US$65.

Once a child is in the custody of the broker, the journey across the rural West African landscape is often dangerous. Many children die in transit and are discarded along the way. Brokers pay minimal fares and expenses during the children's journey as well as required bribes to ensure the collaboration of border guards and officials. Brokers will recoup their money and much more from the direct labor or sexual exploitation of the child, or by selling the child to another individual at an average mark-up of 250% of the total expense associated with the child. Children exploited for labor are typically forced to work 18 hour days, seven days a week without rest and are either chained to their work position or are locked in the work compound. Children sexually exploited, are primarily involved in brothel or street prostitution, but with the advent of technology have been exploited as subjects of sexually explicit photographs and videos that have been distributed via the Internet in e-mails and on pornographic websites. A significant number of child slaves run away, but are unable to return home or find mainstream employment and as a result resort to living on the street as panhandlers, street prostitutes or become thieves of opportunity. In 2005 it was estimated that 80 million children under the age of 14 were in slavery worldwide.

Having obtained as much information as I could through my research at arms length, I made the decision to pursue my inquiries further and arrange to meet Bill personally in Cotonou, Benin. The flight had me spend a little over 14 hours before the Air France aircraft touched down at Cotonou Airport. I had traveled well over 5,000 miles, clear across the earth to a world the majority of North Americans had seldom seen or even knew existed. Walk up to any passerby in downtown Washington, Los Angeles, Toronto or Ottawa and ask them if they know where Cotonou or even Benin is. You will soon realize how insulated the majority of people are from the people and goings on in their own world. Yet it is the faceless, unknown people in places like these that are often enslaved to produce mass market consumer items for fashion conscious western consumers who readily pay tens of thousands of percentage points over what an entire child labor force would see in even a year from their toils. As I made my way through the terminal, I noted a security check point for a local charter air service manned by, for lack of a better description, civilian security personnel. What made this observation stick in my mind was the level of professionalism and seriousness they brought to their duty while "wanding" each passenger before they boarded in search of weapons or knives; with handheld Tandy (Radio Shack) stud sensors originally designed for use in home renovations.

I met up with Bill the next day at my hotel, the Drake Cotonou Hotel. We enjoyed a light lunch in the hotel café as Bill provided an updated situation report on what we had covered in our numerous communiqués over the previous months. He told me that Diettmarr was very active in the region procuring young girls and that due to a lack of manpower, corruption and cross-jurisdictional activities, how, based on his experience of years as an observer that it was unlikely that this individual would ever be stopped as a child slave broker, let alone be apprehended. I couldn't get the image of the little girl that I had happened across months before out of my mind, and as a result led me to this place.

The following day, Bill arranged to give me a tour of the area and offered to introduce me to some of the families who had their children taken from them by men such as Diettmarr. As well, he introduced me to some of the children who had been fortunate enough to be rescued from the streets having escaped the clutches of labor and sexual exploitive task masters. During my day long tour I met with no less than four families who had their daughters abducted while playing outside their home. I met about a dozen children ranging in age from 10 to 15 who had managed to run away from their keepers. The children in most cases, taken from their families as young as 6 never really knew their parents or where home might be. However, they felt that there had to be more to life than being ruled over by a task master and decided to run away, but had no plan or idea where. As with many child slaves, life on the street was yet another form of slavery, but for many, at least even street life offered more freedom. These children now lived in an orphanage and fortunate for them, received basic schooling and care that they would have not received otherwise. While the children behaved in a very polite manner, it was apparent that most were afraid of me, a new face, because of previous trauma in their lives.

Two of the older girls however, told me of their experiences. The girls had been taken from their home and had been thrown in the back of a truck in chains with other girls, all lying on the floor on top of each other. They spent two or three days in the truck, being only given small amounts of water and fruit to share among them. Some girls became very ill and were taken out of the truck and never returned. When they arrived at their destination, the girls were washed and given a clean set of clothes. One of the girls was forced to live and work in a comfort house (brothel) where if she was ever to even step outside of the house she would be beaten with the threat of death. She told me that apart from the usual brothel services, that she would also be required to participate in modeling sessions by herself and with others, while customers would take pictures. The other girl was sent to a labor camp where she was forced to sew buttons on garments, as she put it, for a long time past when she was sleepy. Looking at her small hands, you could see the scars and damage on her fingers from hours of sewing past the point of the pain and bleeding that she had endured. She told of being locked in the factory until all her work was done which could take days. Only after her work was completed would she be allowed to sleep on the floor on a large mat with the other workers.

Bill and the agency he worked for was well known in the area, and he provided me an introduction to a senior constable he knew at a rural police house. The constable, a man in his mid-forties was very polite and democratic in his demeanor with me. He knew what my interest was, but he was careful not to offer anything new that I did not raise in our conversation. The impression I got was that he was there to do only what the minimal requirement was, nothing more, nothing less, but most of all to do it well without creating waves. Considering his "patch" (geographic area of responsibility) I could understand why he didn't want to rock the boat. Especially in a rural area with slave and drug traffickers, gun runners, and corrupt officials.

From discussions with the locals, I learned that Diettmarr was very active in trading female child slaves and was so well known that even socialites all throughout Africa had used his services in acquiring domestic workers. I also learned that Diettmarr dabbled quite often in the sexual exploitation of many of these young girls in the form of photography and videos that he would distribute via an underground network to Europe. There was no doubt in my mind, based on the image I had analyzed, personal testimony I had heard from the locals and aid workers, as well as former child slaves that Diettmarr was a man of little conscience or morality.

During my tour, Bill introduced me to Naim, a boy of about 15 years of age who had been sold to a leader of a local drug trafficking ring. We came across Naim briefly, as he was running errands for the trafficker in the city. Bill had told me that this boy had been sold to the traffickers when he was 10 and had suffered several beatings from his keepers and that many times he spoke to Bill about running away but was afraid of his fate should he run. Bill told me that he could offer the boy safe refuge by sending him to an orphanage in another West African country operated by another agency he had close ties with. However, the boy never got up enough courage to accept. Naim and his other child mates kept by the traffickers would collect money and deliver drugs to various locations.

Frustrated but undaunted by all of this, I decided to pursue my inquiries more on a personal level. It wasn't long before I found myself in a local bar where Diettmarr and his associates were known to frequent. It was there at the bar I met a man who was known as Ivo. Ivo was a very tall, tanned European gentleman. Through making some rather obvious inquiries of the bartender; the bartender, a local, decided to alert Ivo to my interest in child slaves. Of course, the bartender did this because he knew that if I were to enter into a financial arrangement with Ivo that he might receive the benefit of a finder's fee. It wasn't that the bartender was in on the market but simply considered it another way of making some extra cash to support his own family in this impoverished part of the world.

My meeting with Ivo was much more direct and to the point than I was used to. However, it was my intent to use all of my skills and experience in the art of elicitation to obtain as much intelligence (information) as I could in order to put an end to Diettmarr's trading days.

Elicitation also referred to as passive or soft interrogation, social or wet engineering; is the art and science of obtaining information from a person of interest in a non-threatening, ordinary conversation without their knowledge and in some cases planting an idea for them to act on. Elicitation uses four stages to obtain information or action from the unsuspecting target; (i) appeal to the target's ego, (ii) relate to the target by indicating a common bond or mutual interest, (iii) make believable but deliberate false statements relating to the information you really want in order to get responses from your target framed in real facts, and (iv) causing them to consider an action or option solely driven by their ego or self-aggrandizement.

After a few drinks, I soon learned that Ivo was one of Diettmarr's scouts, and although he gave the impression that he was the sole author of his own actions, it became apparent that he was simply a facilitator under Diettmarr's direction. I learned a great deal about the operation, its locations and baited Ivo with the idea that I was interested in acquiring two or three teenaged boys to take back home with me to use as factotums. I also learned that Diettmarr kept a comfort house (brothel) where he had young girls entertain male customers and also perform as models for Internet photography. Based on the information I had obtained, progressively over our three hour meeting which seemed to go by as if only an hour; my plan on how I would dismantle this operation became clearer. Ivo and I parted company with an arrangement to meet again, after he consulted with Diettmarr and to allow me to make my arrangements in receiving two boys.

The following day, I had to move fast. I accidentally, but on purpose arranged to see Naim in the downtown market where he was known to do his rounds. Although time was a luxury neither of us had, my mission was to get this boy out of the clutches of his keepers but in order to do this, I would have to gain his trust and confidence, in this, only the second time we had ever met. After re-establishing my initial introduction to him via Bill, a person he trusted and respected, I started off with a conjuring trick, with the opening line, "can I show you something?" One of the greatest honors in my life was knowing and having the opportunity to receive lessons in conjuring from some of the greatest magicians of our time. These magicians may not have been in the public spotlight but were what many magic historians would refer to as "magicians' magicians." These were the illusionists that developed, wrote, modified and provided illusions for the magicians that had become household names in the latter half of the last century. My acquaintance with them will always be cherished.

For Naim, I performed the Classic Coin Transportation and my own version of Hot Rod. Naim's eyes lit up with wonder and in a place where children never get to be children, and magic is only a fable, I could see that for a brief moment, he experienced a freedom he never knew before. Our conversation soon came back to reality but I felt and he knew that together we could get him out safely. Having his commitment that he was indeed going to follow through, I asked him where he and the other boys gathered to collect the drugs before making their runs. He was very hesitant to divulge this, but with much persuasion on my part I was able to get a time and place.

After my meeting with Naim, I stopped by Bill's office. I made it look more like a social call but I told Bill that I had found a young boy and a few of his mates that I would like him to make arrangements for at an out of country orphanage and that they would need safe but swift passage. Bill was curious as to the identity of the boy, but I told him that I did not know the boy's name but that he had approached me at my hotel and needed our help to run from his keepers. Bill agreed to arrange this and have his resources on standby for me.

While making my initial rounds throughout the rural regions, I had noticed a base camp for a private security firm that had been engaged by a western transport company in order to reduce looting and piracy of the trucks bringing goods throughout the region. Private security companies such as these are contracted to locations throughout the third and second world where law enforcement resources are minimal at best. The men and women who provide these services are typically former career soldiers who face high risk situations daily in order to maintain safety, security and order for those in their charge. To those in the safe, secure and comfort of their home in the west, they are quick to dismiss these individuals as mercenaries or soldiers of fortune, but to the rest of the world they are simply professional soldiers who represent a very fragile thin line between order and chaos. I entered the compound and introduced myself to one of the men doing some work around a deuce and a half (2 ½ ton truck). I asked him if I could speak to the officer in charge. He pointed his finger in the direction of a trailer, which I walked towards. I entered the trailer and amidst the makeshift unfinished rough wood tables and shelves with maps, manuals, charts and folders covering most of the surfaces, I was met by a late-50ish gentleman of rotund stature of about 5 feet, with the stub of a previously enjoyed cigar in his mouth. He looked up and asked, "What do you want?" I introduced myself and asked him if he was in charge of the security team. He in turn introduced himself simply as "Mike" and told me he was in charge.

I noticed that on his desk was a grey marble block with the regimental cap badge of the Governor General's Horse Guards. I decided to try my hand at a rapport exercise with him, as I had a really big favor to ask him and figured I needed all the help I could get. I looked at it and said, "So, were you in the GGHG?" Surprised, his attention on me seemed more focused and he said, "Now what do you know about the GGHG?" I knew I had him, but just had to work it the right way. I told him I recalled some found memories of my time with the reservists of the GGHG at Dennison Armoury back in Canada and how it had been a shame that in later years they decided to demolish and rebuild Dennison. I spoke of found memories, of friendships and comradeship found and lost; things that only a soldier could relate to. He looked at me and said, "Well, I wasn't a GGHG but my son was. He gave me this thing and I just lug it around for luck."

We exchanged some war stories, and I found out that he hailed from Moose Jaw, Saskatchewan; home of 15 Wing and 431 Squadron (Snowbirds Demonstration Team). Having exhausted the pleasantries, I moved the conversation towards why I came to Benin. Mike listened intently but looked skeptical. Nonetheless, I continued and then, in a matter of fact tone, I asked him if he could do me a favor and see if any of his men would be willing to do guard duty for about 4 hours at two locations while I relocated some children to a transport bound for an orphanage. To my surprise, Mike said, "No, I won't ask them. You tell me how many men you need and where it is, and we'll be there." At that point, with the pressure off my shoulders for this part of my mission, I could breathe a little easier. Our meeting ended with a shot of Drambuie and as I drove away I couldn't help but feel that we were going to make some real changes in the morning.

That evening, I met Ivo in the bar. I told him that I was leaving the country tomorrow evening and that I wanted two children delivered to me, at my hotel no later than 1800 hours. Ivo looked upset at my demand but his ego made him not want to admit that it would be near impossible for him to get me two boys by then. So, using my social engineering skills, I put him in a situation where I told him how he could get some boys for me and that if he didn't feel that he could handle it or he was intimidated by the money I was offering that we could both agree that I had been dealing with the wrong person all along. Of course, he accepted the challenge. The next day would be extremely risky for everyone concerned, but it was a risk that I was personally willing to take. However, by my own admission, retrospectively now, it was a risk that I put on many without their knowledge. In the back of my mind, I justified this at the time by risking the few in an attempt to save the many future children that would be the victims of Diettmarr and his gang.

It came as no surprise that, coincidentally, Ivo and his gang of child rustlers arrived at a rendezvous point where Naim and three other children were exchanging drugs and money for their overseers. Of course, Ivo and his men had no idea who these children belonged to or what they had. As predicted greed dictated that all of the children be scooped up by Ivo and his men without much of a fight. They headed to the outskirts of the city. The four children bounced around in the back of a canvas covered pick-up, chained to the floor. As the sun began to blossom at sunrise, Ivo's vehicle was met by six heavily armed masked individuals who happened to hijack Ivo's vehicle; leaving him and his men to fend for themselves. The hijackers, were of course, compliments of Mike and Naim and his friends were released from their chains and handed over to Bill who had arranged to get them settled in an out of country orphanage.

Mike's men and I arranged to get Ivo's vehicle back to its parking space in the city. We arranged to have the drugs and money placed in the vehicle that Diettmarr was known to drive. We used makeshift bags made out of burlap coffee sacks to hold the drugs and cash, and then attached them under the wheel wells of his vehicle using old surplus aircraft magnets. We took a big risk while doing this, but were successful.

Just as Ivo had told me inadvertently, it didn't take long for Diettmarr and his two other remaining men to head out in search of new children that morning right on schedule. However, today was not going to be his day. An old man, a local had got word to the local Drug Lord that his property had been interfered with by Diettmarr's men, and that Ivo had been seen rounding up his slaves.

As soon as Diettmarr left and allowing for enough time and distance, I took Mikes' men with me to the comfort house (brothel) that Diettmarr operated in the city's outskirts. We approached the run down four room, single level house with extreme caution. At that point, I along with six members of Mike's team stormed the brothel where we only encountered an elderly lady, the den mother and seven children ranging in age from about 10 to 15, with three patrons running half dressed out of the backdoor.

There was a room with video and photographic equipment with small holes cut in the walls where videos and still images were made of what transpired in the adjoining rooms between children and patrons. On the walls were photographs of children, at least 40 or so, and it was there that I had seen a photograph of the scared little girl that brought me here. Written on the back of it was the name Rispah. I didn't recall seeing her in the group of children we gathered at this house. I asked the older girls if they knew her and one girl Anise, told me that they were friends but Rispah became very ill and that she had died in her sleep and was thrown in the river just over a year ago. I was too late for Rispah, but little did she know that she would be the reason for the liberation of her friends.

All of the children were placed in our truck and delivered to Bill who had arranged for safe passage to an out of country orphanage, where they could at least be children again, receive an education and perhaps even be reunited with their family.

That day, Bill, Naim, Mike and his team all did an extraordinary thing. They saved eleven children, and it was only 1500 hours! The day wasn't quite over.

I went back to my hotel and got cleaned up, and pondered the events that transpired. Forgetting what time it was, I wandered into the bar and decided to order something to eat. As I sat there, in deep contemplation looking out the window, two dark green police pick-up trucks drove by with bodies piled on their flatbeds barely covered with undersized blue tarpaulins. In the back of my mind I knew the answer but offered a puzzled look to the bartender, who always knew what was happening, and who was doing what to whom. He looked back at me with a rather suspicious look in his eye and said, "That's Diettmarr, Ivo and his gang. They stole drugs, money and slaves from the drug man here, and he didn't like it. You shouldn't mess with the drug man because luck can only go so far."

Today was the day that Diettmarr's child slave trade and child sexploitation ended for good. Even though I knew that he was only one of hundreds and that there would be someone ready to take his place, it was a good day as far as I was concerned and it was time to head home.

▼

CONSTRUCTION PLANS FOR NEHASA'S RADIO (VARIOMETER RADIO)

If you have basic mechanical and electronic skills you can build the same battery-less shortwave radio that I built for Nehasa I wrote about in Chapter 5. This radio is actually an advanced version of a crystal radio and is known as a Variometer Radio because it uses what is known as the Variometer Principle of a continuously variable inductor for tuning in stations.

If you live in an urban area with several AM radio stations you may find that these signals are so strong that they may be the only ones you might receive on this radio due to overloading. However, take comfort in the fact that you actually built something from absolute scratch that works! On the other hand if you are having problems receiving stations, try adjusting the location of the antenna and double check to be sure that the ground connection is good.

Parts List
D1–1N34 germanium diode
C1, C3–100 picofarad ceramic disc capacitor
C2–0.001 microfarad ceramic disc capacitor
L1, L3–90 tightly wound turns of number 22 gauge enameled wire around a 1-inch diameter plastic or cardboard tube
L2–81 tightly wound turns of number 22 gauge enameled wire around a 1.5-inch diameter plastic or cardboard tube
T1—Audio Output Transformer 1K ohm to 8 ohms
EAR—High Impedance or Crystal Earpiece or Headphones (put alligator clips on ends)
14-inch x 10-inch x 0.25-inch thick wood or plastic Chef's cutting board
1–3-inch strap hinge
10–1.5-inch bolts with matching nuts and washers
15–0.5-inch bolts with matching nuts and washers
150 feet of 22 gauge enameled wire
50 feet of 16 gauge insulated stranded hook-up wire
1–8.5-inch, 1-inch diameter plastic or cardboard tube
1–4-inch, 2-inch diameter plastic or cardboard tube
2—small plastic (not metal) corner brackets
1–8.5-inch, 1-inch diameter wooden dowel rod (flatten one side of this slightly with sandpaper)
6–1-inch alligator clips
1—bottle of clear nail polish or tube of household cement
1—sheet medium grit sandpaper

NEHASA'S RADIO

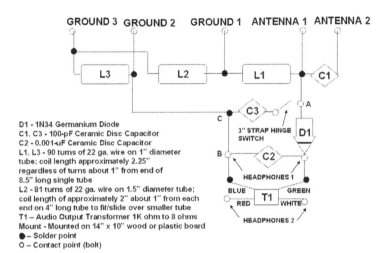

GROUND 3 GROUND 2   GROUND 1   ANTENNA 1 ANTENNA 2

L3   L2   L1   C1

D1 - 1N34 Germanium Diode
C1, C3 - 100-pF Ceramic Disc Capacitor
C2 - 0.001-uF Ceramic Disc Capacitor
L1, L3 - 90 turns of 22 ga. wire on 1" diameter
tube; coil length approximately 2.25"
regardless of turns about 1" from end of
8.5" long single tube
L2 - 81 turns of 22 ga. wire on 1.5" diameter tube;
coil length of approximately 2" about 1" from each
end on 4" long tube to fit/slide over smaller tube
T1 – Audio Output Transformer 1K ohm to 8 ohms
Mount - Mounted on 14" x 10" wood or plastic board
● – Solder point
O – Contact point (bolt)

C3   A
C
3" STRAP HINGE   D1
SWITCH
B   C2
HEADPHONES 1
BLUE   T1   GREEN
RED   WHITE
HEADPHONES 2

Let's build it.

1. Carefully study the pictures to see the general layout of all the parts and how everything is connected. The black dots indicate permanent connection points which may be soldered or bolted securely in place. The open dots with the exception where the hinge switch is used are connection points where the 1.5-inch bolts are used, in order to allow the operator to connect antennas, ground wires and headphones using alligator clips.

2. Take the 8.5-inch tube and put small holes large enough to run the enameled wire through, at the following points measuring from the end of the tube 0.5-inches, 1-inch, 3.25-inches, 5.25-inches, 7.5-inches and 8-inches.

3. Take the 4-inch tube and put a small hole large enough to run the enameled wire through, at the following points measuring from the end of the tube 0.5-inches, 1-inch, 3-inches and 3.5-inches.

4. Take the 8.5-inch tube and a roll of number 22 enamel wire and place the end of the wire through the hole at the 1-inch mark from the end (the second hole) and then feed it back up through the hole at the 0.5-inch mark from the end (the first hole). Be sure that you have approximately 5-inches of the wire coming outside of the hole. Now gently twist the loose end of the wire around the other end coming out of the hole connected to the roll to secure it in place. Now start tightly winding the wire around the tube, placing each wire wind beside the other and not overlapping. Do this until you count a total of 90 winds. Then snip the roll approximately 10-inches from the coil and push the loose end through the hole at the 3.25-inch mark (the third hole) on the tube and then guide it through the tube to the hole at the 0.5-inch mark (the first hole) and feed it up through the hole and then push the end inside the tube and back up through the hole again to secure the end. The wire should be pretty much tight, flush against the tube.

5. Take the 8.5-inch tube and a roll of number 22 enamel wire and place the end of the wire through the hole at the 7.5-inch mark from the end (the fifth hole) and then feed it back up through the hole at the 8-inch mark from the end (the sixth hole). Be sure that you have approximately 5-inches of the wire coming

outside of the hole. Now gently twist the loose end of the wire around the other end coming out of the hole connected to the roll to secure it in place. Now start tightly winding the wire around the tube, placing each wire wind beside the other and not overlapping. Do this until you count a total of 90 winds. Then snip the roll approximately 10-inches from the coil and push the loose end through the hole at the 5.25-inch mark (the fourth hole) on the tube and then guide it through the tube to the hole at the 8-inch mark (the sixth hole) and feed it up through the hole and then push the end inside the tube and back up through the hole again to secure the end. The wire should be pretty much tight, flush against the tube.

6. Take the 4-inch tube and a roll of number 22 enamel wire and place the end of the wire through the hole at the 1-inch mark from the end (the second hole) and then feed it back up through the hole at the 0.5-inch mark from the end (the first hole). Be sure that you have approximately 3-inches (14-inches) of the wire coming outside of the hole. Now gently twist the loose end of the wire around the other end coming out of the hole connected to the roll to secure it in place. Now start tightly winding the wire around the tube, placing each wire wind beside the other and not overlapping. Do this until you count a total of 81 winds. Then snip the roll approximately 3-inches from the coil and push the loose end through the hole at the 3-inch mark (the third hole) on the tube and then guide it through the tube to the hole at the 3.5-inch mark (the fourth hole) and feed it up through the hole and then push the end

inside the tube and back up through the hole again to secure the end. The wire should be pretty much tight, flush against the tube.

7. Take the bottle of clear nail polish or tube of household cement and put a light coating on all three coils you have just finished. Be sure cover all the windings evenly. This will protect the windings from coming loose. Be sure to let them dry completely for at least 24 hours.

8. Using sandpaper, sand approximately 0.5-inch to 0.75-inch of the ends of the coils you wound. You must be sure to remove all of the enamel coating in order to make a good electrical connection.

9. Cut off 2–14-inch sections of insulated hook-up wire and remove about 0.75-inches of insulation from both ends of each section. Solder one end of each section to the enamel wires of the 4-inch tube.

10. Review the pictures to see the layout of all the parts and how to wire the components together. It is important to note that most of the wiring is done on top of the board with only 5 connections made under the board (see photo). These connections are marked A, B, C and Antenna 1, Ground 2. All wiring above and below the board is done using the insulated hook-up wire. The enamel wire is only used for the coils and is much too fragile for the remainder of this project.

11. Take a pencil and mark out on your board where everything should go based on the pictures and then set the actual components you have on the board to be

sure they have enough spacing and room. Once you are satisfied, you can drill your holes, and start loose-fitting your bolts in place.

12. Insert the wooden dowel rod inside the 8.5-inch tube, with the side you flattened (see the parts list) towards the wires inside the tube. Slide the 4-inch tube over the 8.5-inch tube. Now use the small plastic corner brackets to mount this assembly onto the board once you are ready.

13. To make the antenna wire for the radio cut off an 18-foot section of hook-up wire and remove about 0.75-inches of insulation from both ends of each section. Attach an alligator clip to each end of the section.

14. To make the ground wire for the radio cut off an 18-foot section of hook-up wire and remove about 0.75-inches of insulation from both ends of each section. Attach an alligator clip to each end of the section.

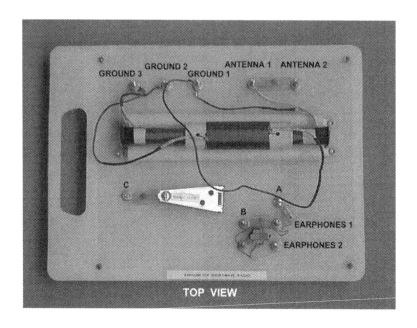

TOP VIEW

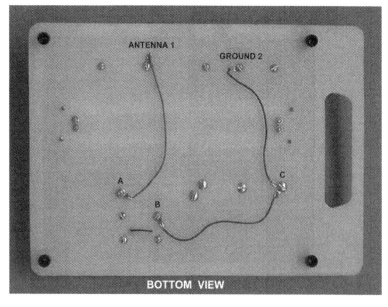

BOTTOM VIEW

Let's Use It:

1. Attach one end of the ground wire to a radiator, heating vent, pipe or facet. You may have to use sandpaper to remove paint or rust in order to make good electrical contact. If you are using this radio outdoors, drive a 9" to 12" metal spike or metal tent peg into the ground with about 1" exposed above the ground and attach one end of your ground wire to this. Attach the other end of the ground wire to the bolt on your radio marked Ground 1.

2. Attach one end of the antenna wire to the bolt on your radio marked Antenna 1. Take the other end of the antenna wire and loop the end around two of your fingers and clip the alligator clip into the insulation to make an oval loop. Hang the antenna by the loop on the wall or if outdoors, to a medium height tree branch or any other non-metallic support at least 6' above the ground.

3. Attach your earphones or headphones to the bolts on your radio marked Headphones 1 or Headphones 2. Depending on the type you use, one or the other contact will work. Just listen carefully to hear if you hear static of any kind. If you do, this is the best connection point.

4. Tune in the stations by sliding the 4-inch tube slowly and carefully across the 8.5-inch tube. When you do this be sure that you are touching only the tube not the wire coil as you will reduce the performance of your radio.

5. By changing the ground connection to either Ground 1, 2 or 3 and antenna connection to either Antenna 1 or 2; you are changing the operating band of the radio. Depending on where you are located, you can experiment to see what combination best "pulls in" the signals for you.

6. Once you have found the best antenna and ground combination and tuned in a station by using the slider tube, you may be able to even further improve reception by closing or opening the hinge (switch) which will add some additional "fine" tuning.

7. If you are having problems with reception after having double checked all your connections and tried all the different antenna, ground and headphone combinations; try moving the entire radio to another room. It sounds odd but it actually works. Bear in mind that this radio is powered by the radio signals it is actually picking up in the air, nothing else. So if the signal can't get in, it cannot work.

8. If you get tired of using headphones or earphones you can get a pair of inexpensive amplified computer speakers, carefully cut the audio plug off of them, remove about 0.75-inches of insulation off of the ends of the wire where the plug used to be and hook them up to either the Headphones 1 or 2 contact point on your radio. Of course this defeats the purpose of having a radio that doesn't rely on electricity but you can still have bragging rights as you let everyone in the room listen to a radio that you built from scratch.

APPENDIX B

▼

WE HAVE THE TECHNOLOGY TO STOP CHILD PORNOGRAPHY

Child Pornography is the photographing, filming, videotaping, artistic rendering or writing of explicit or implied sexual activity of children, the final product of these acts and the activity of distributing these items. On a worldwide basis, Child Pornography generated approximately US$3 billion in 2004 (CDN$4 billion, GBP 2 billion). While Child Pornography has existed throughout history, the introduction of technology such as the Internet, digital image technology and storage has fostered the exponential growth of this crime. There are paedophiles and organized child sex rings that thrive off of, and propagate this crime without regard or remorse for their victims. The typical age range of their victims is from 3 to 12 years of age. The act of Child Pornography sees the innocent trust of an unknowing child betrayed, a child coerced or tricked into an abusive situation, or a child threatened with violence in order to perform. The scars left on a child from these acts will last a lifetime.

Five percent of all adult Internet traffic contains some form of Child Pornography while three percent of adult websites offer access to illegal Child Pornography. Each day approximately 75 million e-mails worldwide contain some form of Child Pornography and each month approximately 45 million files are downloaded or shared worldwide. In September 2005, the term "Child Pornography" was searched an average of 1,957 times per day worldwide using Internet search engines with approximately 6,540,000 websites indexed and accessible through these search engines using this key phrase.

Today, the major challenge for law enforcement in stopping Child Pornography and Child Pornographers lies in the ability to identify the perpetrators and distribution of this material. Given the limited resources available, law enforcement has been able to make some gains in reducing Child Pornography. The trend by most governments is to legislate Internet Service Providers into filtering content so that Child Pornography doesn't reach subscribers computers and to report subscribers that may be suspect. Furthermore, sentencing of Child Pornographers is seldom in tune with the crime and its impact on society. Most white collar crimes will carry stiffer penalties than a crime of child pornography. While this shields the public and restricts access and distribution for low level pornographers it does very little to apprehend those directly involved at the source of manipulating the world's children.

However, the major governments of the world have the technology in place to shut down 60% to 70% of Child Pornography on the Internet and identify those responsible. The problem lies in political will and receiving the mandate to do so.

In 1971 a system known as ECHELON was established by the United States, the United Kingdom, Canada, Australia and New Zealand. The purpose of ECHELON was and still is today, to monitor and intercept global communications for the purpose of national security interests between the five countries. Using supercomputers and skilled intelligence analysts, the system monitors 3 billion communications daily including telephone calls, e-mail messages, Internet downloads, satellite transmissions, video transmissions and several other communications modalities. Regardless of whether the communication is sent by radio waves, cable, fibre or infrared; ECHELON has the capability to "listen in." The system monitors all of the world's communications indiscriminately and then filters out or selects specific transmissions based on keyword phrases, digital signatures, digital image values and other preprogrammed criteria using a combination of artificial intelligence, fuzzy logic and the power of supercomputers.

It is not surprising that ECHELON routinely monitors 90% of all of the world's Internet traffic. With this capability alone, ECHELON could intercept and identify 67 million e-mails containing Child Pornography on a daily basis and track these back to the originator and recipient. This action alone, if properly followed up would lock down the Internet and lock out 60% of the distribution of Child Pornography world wide, leading to the arrest of those involved. ECHELON is the largest signals intelligence (SIGINT) system in the world. In addition, there are smaller, national systems of similar capability operated in the United States, the United Kingdom, Canada, Australia, New Zealand, the European Union, Russia, China, Germany, Israel, France and India.

In a perfect world, ECHELON and these smaller national SIGINT (Signals Intelligence) systems would be utilized to aid law enforcement in the war on Child Pornography. But sadly, this is not the case. The United States government refuses to officially, publicly acknowledge that ECHELON exists while the other four countries involved in the system have accepted the fact that the majority of their citizens know about the system in general terms but are not forthcoming on any other information regarding these systems that their citizens pay for via their taxes.

As of 20 June 2005 I had assembled a petition consisting of well over 5 million signatories from around the globe that reflected my efforts of a full year of lobbying and mobilizing the world's Internet community in an effort to use this untapped resource to save the world's children from being victims of Child Pornography. While some may balk at this mere 5 million, it has been quite an accomplishment considering that despite my own personal activities in the North American mainstream broadcast media, this initiative received virtually no promotion or mention in the North American broadcast or print media. Sadly, it simply was not newsworthy enough. This petition was digitally presented on this same date to the five sovereign signatories involved in ECHELON to urge them to use this system in the identification of Child Pornography and as an aid to local law enforcement in the apprehension of Child Pornographers. It is my sincerest hope, that this initiative, dubbed "The Ing Initiative" may be given consideration by the world's governments.

I began this initiative because I believed and still believe that it is better to take a stand on an issue rather than leave it alone because it may not be popular, politically correct or that someone else or government should take care of it. I hope that you will consider joining me.

Whether you have participated in my petition or are just learning about this initiative, it is still not too late. Please write your local federal government representative and tell him or her how you feel about Child Pornography.

We have the technology to stop Child Pornography. Let's use it!

Please visit my main website to learn more about me and my activities regarding technology crime at www.drroberting.com

APPENDIX C

▼

WHERE I STAND

As a result of my appearances on national television, being a featured speaker at public events and having hosted several documentaries I have been asked about my political philosophy or where I stand on various social and political issues.

I don't subscribe to any one political (party) line although many people aren't happy until they try to put me into one of those little boxes. I am a firm believer in "responsibility to the responsible." I believe that many people who run for public office do so to simply get elected rather than to establish a firm mandate, to actually stand for something that they believe in. So, at the risk of being unpopular but standing firmly on what I believe and accepting full responsibility for this stand, here are the top 18 issues that I feel strongly about and my abridged perspective on them.

1. I stand for Capital Punishment (the death sentence) for individuals who knowingly take the life of another human

being, and for those who commit physical sexual assault (rape); in situations where the allegations of such an offense are clearly substantiated by scientific and direct evidence. As well, I believe that those who directly commit capital crimes must be tried equitably regardless of age. Anyone capable of such heinous acts regardless of age have clearly demonstrated their capacity and capability to commit (and commit again) such an act. However, it must be established beyond doubt that the accused was indeed directly responsible for the alleged act; something our current judicial system is incapable of doing.

2. I stand for a Work Fair Program; a program where those completely supported by welfare or social assistance must earn their stipend by volunteer work in the community of not less than 20 hours per week. The only exception to this would be those recipients that are certified as medically unfit by a physician. Single mothers who live alone with their children would be required to either do 8 hours of out-of-home volunteer work or do equivalent work at home (telephoning or stuffing envelopes for a charity from home). No community work, no check.

3. I stand for effective immigration policies that would provide zero tolerance of persons entering or residing in our country illegally. Immigration, as is citizenship in our country is a privilege unless provided by birth, and I would disqualify any immigration applicant that has a violent or sexual offender criminal record; the barring of organized crime, gang or member of a terrorist organization and sympathizers; economic refugees; and those who cannot obtain a legitimate offer of employment or full time enrollment in a recognized educational

institution. People of legal age sponsored as spouses, children or parents must be required to contribute to the community by providing a minimum of 8 hours community service per week for not less than 5 years after landing legally in this country. This would ensure that they become acclimatized to our culture, their community and make them a contributing member of our nation.

4. I stand for effective law enforcement and public safety. I believe that additional funding must be provided for the safety and security of our current front line law enforcement officers in the way of personal protective equipment and training. I believe public law enforcement resources must be directed towards the protection, prevention and apprehension of violent and sexual offenders, organized crime, gangs and terrorist organizations. I believe in the empowerment of law abiding citizens in our communities and would mandate official cooperation and reciprocity between all law enforcement agencies and those community stakeholders such as private security agencies, organized volunteer street patrol and neighborhood watch groups in order to deter and report crime in their neighborhood.

5. I stand for a strong military capable of defending our country on our own soil. Our sons and daughters should be defending our soil not that of a foreign nation. The only role that our military has on another's soil with the exception of responding to a direct attack on our nation; is to provide humanitarian relief, not that of an aggressor or invader. We must support our service people and after they have served their country whether it be for a minimum term or as a career service person it is our

duty in both the public and private sector, and the community to offer the courtesy and respect required to help them integrate back into the community. We must ensure that the people in our military are trained to safely and effectively execute the tasks required of them with the best equipment and support available.

6. I stand for the right to work and education for all legal residents of our country. I believe that mandatory partnerships between government, colleges, universities and the private and public business sector must be established. In order for colleges or universities to receive any form of government funding, subsidy or their students to do so; the institution must have valid agreements with government, the private and public business sectors offering a willingness to employ graduates of their programs. Business will be required to create and join with other business in their industry, an employee resource network where if one company downsizes, those employees may be accessible on a priority basis to another firm in the same industry requiring experienced employees. For people that find themselves unemployed and want to work, despite best efforts on their part to secure employment, I believe that a government funded Employment Corps program should be established that will utilize the skills and experience of these individuals regardless of age at fair market value, so that they can contribute to their community and our country. While we have a public school system, subsidized through tax dollars, I feel that this does not go far enough. I believe that any student who is a citizen of our country, from a middle to low income family who receives an 80% average upon Secondary School graduation should receive a one time, first year 100% "citizenship"

scholarship towards any full time academic or vocational program of their choice.

7. I stand for elected public figures regardless of what level of government, to be in the service of the public and be remunerated as such. All too often elected officials vote themselves raises using the reasoning that they must be on par with their corporate counterparts, while telling the citizens that elected them to "tighten their belts" because we have a deficit. I say no more. All too many citizens are robbed of time with their families because they must work two or more jobs just to survive. Elected officials should not be paid any more than 25% above the average wage of the people they serve. Any monies saved by this single budgetary action should be divided up equally and applied towards the public debt, healthcare, education and employment. Furthermore, if any public leader proposes in their budget any cuts to healthcare, education or public safety, it should be made illegal for any politicians to propose, enact or receive an increase in wages or benefits for their service during that budget year.

8. I stand for the legalization and regulation of the adult sex trade industry for the protection of adult sex trade workers and the public. To affirm their rights without prejudice under the law, to ensure public health standards and to reduce the incidence of the under age or exploited in this industry.

9. I stand for the right to personal privacy for all law abiding citizens. Many people in government and in authority have used all forms of equivoque with the cliché "if you have nothing to hide, you should not feel threatened" when they attempt to

legislatively rob the law abiding citizen of their privacy. Even law abiding citizens do have things that they do not wish shared with others or the state; from the things two consenting adults may do legally in the privacy of their own home to their personal social opinions discussed with a close associate. The government, law enforcement, private and public security agencies should not be conducting surveillance, data mining or intelligence gathering on law abiding citizens.

10. I stand for equal legal taxation of individuals and business. Regardless of what personal income level an individual may have, every citizen should be taxed at the same rate with no exceptions. I also believe that this same rule should apply to business. As well, churches and any other religious or not-for-profit organizations deemed as tax exempt that actively partake in lobbying government or activities involving shaping political issues must surrender their tax exempt status and contribute to the system as every other citizen does who has a stake in the government and political system of this country. If you do not contribute to the government or political system of our country as a taxpayer stakeholder, you should not expect the privilege to lobby for, or to be an agent of political or legislative change or reformation.

11. I stand for charity beginning at home. I believe that charity does begin at home and that our government, cannot with clear conscience, send millions of (taxpayer) aid dollars outside of our country when any of our citizens struggle with poverty on a daily basis, our children go hungry, we have working poor, health care deficits, and our First Nations people continue to live in third world conditions in parts of our country. If a

foreign country requires assistance, direct financial support must come from that particular ethnic community and the private sector as a free will donation. The government will, if deemed necessary, commit tax relief for contributions, coordinate delivery of the contributed resources to legitimate representatives and if severe enough, provide a contingent of military personnel for humanitarian relief work if invited by the foreign nation to do so. However, no taxpayer dollars should be directly sent to sustain a foreign nation or its nationals.

12. I stand for better representation and participation of our First Nations peoples throughout all levels of government. The original and true people of this continent have long been neglected and not afforded the courtesy and respect they deserve. I stand for increasing understanding and dialogue on Native issues and soliciting their active participation in shaping the future of our nation as equal stakeholders with all citizens of our country.

13. I stand for respect of the beliefs and cultures of all the people that make up our world. However, I also stand for the protection of our culture, while being respectful to others of different cultures within our nation. We cannot and should not compromise our cultural heritage under the guise of political correctness or an attempt at being optically accommodating to other cultures. We must preserve our cultural heritage, as we expect peoples of other cultures to do the same within their own nation and home. Our nation is our house, and when guests come over, we ask them to respect our house rules (culture) and we in turn respect theirs when in their house (nation). Unfortunately, our cultural heritage has been traded for

political correctness. I embrace, respect and welcome cultural diversity in our country. However, as an example, I believe that we should not be removing the morning Lord's Prayer in public schools, we should not have a debate over the correctness of Christmas Trees in public places or using the phrase "Merry or Happy Christmas", the removal of playing of the National Anthem in schools and at all public events, and we should not have the introduction of non-North American religious laws and judiciary as part of our legal system. Our Western culture was built on a foundation of Christian values, English and French culture. Rightly or wrongly, we must respect, uphold and safeguard our cultural heritage as this was and is the bedrock on which our nation was built. We must preserve this for future generations.

14. I stand for Second Chance legislation for first time non-violent, non-sexual offenders. In our society we have individuals that for whatever the reason, call it plain stupidity, find themselves with a criminal record for a single, one time non-violent criminal conviction that will follow them for life. As a result they meet with great disadvantage when it comes to employment, education, housing and even financial services. Now, let me point out that I am talking about one time offenders of crimes that do not involve any form of violence, rape, abuse against women or children, sex crimes, firearms, weapons, or explosives. It is my belief that if such an individual has served their sentence and has only a single conviction that they should not be discriminated against for a stupid mistake in their past. If we want to curb the tide of criminal repeat offenders, we must make it easier for one time non-violent offenders to reintegrate into society. The quickest way to create

a repeat offender is to set them loose in public with limited employment and housing prospects based on a past mistake. Non-violent one time offenders deserve a one time second chance. I believe in non-discriminatory legislation that would ensure a non-violent first time offender who has completed the requirements of their sentence be afforded the courtesy of re-entering society as an equal stakeholder in the community.

15. I stand for environmental and ecological responsibility. I believe in practical legislated energy conservation standards for all public and private building owners and operators. Standards such as the mandatory use of energy conserving illumination, automatic switches that turn off lights and regulate environmental systems when areas are vacant, the limiting of illuminated outdoor signage with the goal of reducing energy consumption and light pollution and the mandatory installation of water efficient fixtures. I believe that we must promote the development and utilization of passive renewable energy and recycling programs. We must focus on a practical strategy of emissions control whether that source be from automobiles or industry. When it comes to reducing automobile emissions in cities, our goal should not be to centralize commerce in one area, where vehicles are gridlocked burning fuel and then penalize citizens unless they use an over-extended or inadequate public transit system. Rather, in the interest of the environment, we must offer incentives to decentralize development, so that commute times whether by automobile or public transit are reduced, thus reducing emissions and fuel consumption. Highway and road maintenance or utility work involving the closing of a single traffic lane with the exception of emergency repairs must be

executed during off peak hours in order to reduce grid lock and unnecessary fuel consumption and emissions. Taxes or tolls levied on transportation systems should and must be applied directly towards the maintenance, upgrading and increasing the environmental efficiency of these systems. We must protect our green spaces that are inhabited by wildlife in our urban areas. There are many environmental and ecological concerns that must be addressed that for years have been neglected and it is my position that we must address these directly by action not by forming committees or study groups. The studies are in, it is now time for action.

16. I stand for elections at all levels of government to be by paper ballot and manual hand count. While electronic voting systems may offer advantages, the integrity of such systems cannot be easily validated by lay observers, and as such lack the necessary authentication required to ensure security or confidence, much less the trust of the electorate.

17. I stand for increased funding and deployment of preventative medicine programs. Programs that provide the education and equipment for early diagnosis and detection of disease. Programs that ensure timely access to this equipment and professionals. Mandatory programs that teach in our high schools and in first year community/vocational colleges and university programs; nutrition, CPR and first aid, healthy lifestyle choices and accident prevention. Programs that increase public awareness on nutrition, CPR and first aid, healthy lifestyle choices and accident prevention.

18. I stand for government accountability. A government that tells the people who elected it, the facts, not hyperbole. A government that doesn't try to please everybody but one that gets things done, and at the end of the day is clear where it stands on the issues in word and deed.

I have presented my position on these issues in the hope that people everywhere in our country will discuss and consider these issues. These represent only one man's view, mine and no one else's. I will entertain any or all offers of political appointment or nomination!

NEVER GIVE UP.

NEVER SURRENDER.

GLOSSARY

Back Channels: [Intel] A methodology that bypasses routine or established procedures.

Backstop: [Intel, Security] An instructive code computer virus that can be programmed to search for, and e-mail a copy of all files on the targeted computer that have a specific name or keyword phrase to the virus originator.

Briefing: [Intel] A meeting with the intelligence team that reviews the situation report (SitRep), the tasking (METL) for the assignment, the objectives of the project and introduces any external resources that may be deployed. See Debriefing and Pre-Briefing.

Case Officer: [Intel] A mid to low level field intelligence officer responsible for the supervision of field agents.

Chatter: [Intel] A term used to describe voice or data transmission activity on a communication line or channel under surveillance.

Close Protection: [CP] Bodyguarding, VIP, Diplomatic or Executive Protection.

CP: [CP] see Close Protection.

CPO: [CP, Security, LE] Certified Protection Officer or Close Protection Officer.

CPP: [Security]   Certified   Protection Professional.

Cracker: [Security, Intel] Criminal Hacker; often erroneously called a Hacker by the public news media. An individual who uses their technical ability to gain unauthorized access, disrupt, disable, vandalize, manipulate, steal or illegally copy information or intellectual property stored or communicated across a computer or communications network. See Hacker.

DLitt: Doctor of Letters, Litterarum Doctor, Litteratus Doctus.

DSc: Doctor of Science.

Debriefing: [Intel] An individual interview with each member of an intelligence team after an assignment in order to gather as much information about the operation from different perspectives and observations in order to identify small details that may be useful in a follow-up investigation or future projects. See Briefing.

FAPSc: Fellow of the Academy of Police Science.

Fringe: [Intel] An area outside of the target surveillance area that can be monitored.

Hacker: [Security, Intel] An individual with technical ability who modifies, re-engineers or experiments with current or old technology for the purpose of improving performance, or improvised capability just to see how far it will go, for the sake of personal curiosity or interest. See Cracker.

Intelligence Analyst: [Intel] An individual with specialized training used to examine information and evidence gathered from various sources for the purpose of interpreting, plotting and profiling the activity of a Target. Intelligence Analysts are seldom deployed in the field.

Intelligence Officer: [Intel] An individual whose job is to obtain, gather and monitor information either directly or through the deployment of a team using physical and technical resources. Also referred to as Agents; Intelligence Officers are the "Secret Agents" portrayed in films.

METL: [Intel] Mission Essential Task List. A detailed step-by-step (to do) list of actionable items with time frames, deadlines and assigned responsible/ accountable individuals required for the execution of a mission (objective).

Pointer Person: [Intel, LE] A person who has information or may be a known direct or indirect associate of a Target. See Target.

Pre-briefing: [Intel] A one-on-one individual meeting with each member of an intelligence team that provides information on the individual's role, situation that will be encountered, special operating procedures and the specific mission goal for the individual. See Briefing.

Privateer: [Intel] An individual with no formal active association to a government agency with specialized skills in intelligence or security who typically works alone and is available for hire by anyone. Privateers can be good guys or bad guys, depending on their own ethics, loyalties and who their client is.

Project Officer: [Intel] A mid to high level intelligence officer responsible for the supervision and coordination of Case Officers. See Case Officer.

SitRep:

[Intel] Situation Report, typically relevant current state and background information.

Target:

[Intel, Security, LE] A person or group of interest in an investigation or intelligence operation. The primary person or their active lieutenants "in crime."

ABOUT THE AUTHOR

Robert Ing, DSc, DLitt, FAPSc
Forensic Intelligence Specialist & Security Advisor

Dr. Robert Ing became an American Police Hall of Fame award recipient in 2001 and is a recognized authority on technical security and investigation. Dr. Ing has given workshops and lectured extensively on forensic intelligence issues under the auspices of the federal governments of the United States and Canada. As a technology crime and forensic intelligence specialist he has, and continues to make frequent appearances on ABC, CBC, CBS, CNN, CTV, NBC, PBS and other major television news and talk networks. He has been the host of several documentaries for public broadcast and host of Channel 81's, "Technology Crime with Dr. Robert Ing," a weekly one hour technology crime news and information program. In 2005 and 2006, Dr. Ing appeared as a guest on North American broadcast news and talk networks at an average of one segment every 10 days.

He developed an electronic counter-surveillance training program for intelligence personnel in hostile environments (1990), authored one of the first white papers alerting the intelligence community to the national security risk of undetectable "backstop" instructive code computer viruses (1995), and developed a special anti-terrorism training program that over the years has been offered as the basis of a workshop for federal law enforcement personnel (1998). As a result of the potential lives saved due to these innovative initiatives, Dr. Ing was nominated for, and received an American Police Hall of Fame award (2001). In 2004–2005 he lobbied the governments of the United States, the United Kingdom, Canada, Australia and New Zealand, armed with a petition of over 5 million signatories in order to convince these governments to utilize the technological resources of each country's intelligence services as an investigative aid in the apprehension of international child pornographers; this proposal was known as the "Ing Initiative."

He has been recognized by both the public and his peers for his forensic science activities in his roles as investigator, instructor and international security advisor in the areas of espionage risk management, identity theft, Internet security, privacy, computer security and Internet crime. Some of the many awards he has received include the Kaufman Humanitarian Award in 1977, Emergency Services Medal in 1984, the Norris R. Browne Memorial Award in 1995, the Venerable Order of Michael in 2001 and the Warrior's Medal in 2005.

Born in East York, Canada, he attended the prestigious Cambridge Academy and later the North American Institute of Police Science and Alabama School of Fingerprinting; institutions that have been associated with some of North America's most notable investigators. He earned his associate's degree in forensic science from Parker-Clinton College in 1973, his bachelor's degree in electrical engineering technology from LaSalle University in 1991; his master's from LaSalle University in 1992; and his Doctor of Science degree from Knightsbridge University in 1994. He is a Fellow of the Academy of Police Science, a Certified Protection Officer, appointed an Adjunct Professor at LaSalle University in 1992 and has been awarded honorary doctorates from the Finsbury Park Institute in 1995 and Augsburg University in 1996.

For more information on Dr. Robert Ing please visit www.drroberting.com.

Robert Ing, DSc, DLitt, FAPSc

*"Ing is the kind of guy you take home to mother …
to keep tabs on your father!"*
—Chuck Montgomery, Metro City Review

*'There's a fine border between the factual and fictional world's of
CSI … Dr. Ing is the border guard."*
—George Samine, Broadcast Journal

"Definitely one of the best in the business."
—Grace Bell, Review-Journal

*"He puts complex technology in a 5 second plain language sound
bite."*
—Joanne Singleton, THE Weekly

"A real life technology action hero."
—Bud Foxx, Videonotes

*"It's a good thing that Dr. Robert Ing is on the right side of the
law."*
—Kim Geddes, CHUM Radio.

"Ing is a forensic spy catcher."
—Eric Lasago, Underground New York

*"Dr. Ing is truly a twenty-first century member of the League of
Extraordinary Gentlemen."*
—Paul B. Hedges, Channel 81 Productions

*"Ing is a technical security privateer who has traveled the world
with letters of marque from governments and major corporations."*
—Bill Merritt, Conspiracy Theory Radio

978-0-595-45589-8
0-595-45589-1

www.ingramcontent.com/pod-product-compliance
Lightning Source LLC
Chambersburg PA
CBHW051230050326
40689CB00007B/864